Duncan Fraser

Riverside rambles of an Edinburgh angler

Duncan Fraser

Riverside rambles of an Edinburgh angler

ISBN/EAN: 9783337374495

Printed in Europe, USA, Canada, Australia, Japan

Cover: Foto ©Lupo / pixelio.de

More available books at **www.hansebooks.com**

RIVERSIDE RAMBLES

OF AN

EDINBURGH ANGLER

BY

DUNCAN FRASER

FIRST PRESIDENT OF THE EDINBURGH SATURDAY ANGLING CLUB

Illustrated by Tom Scott, A.R.S.A.

SELKIRK: GEORGE LEWIS & SON

MDCCCXCV

THE FOLLOWING SKETCHES

ARE INSCRIBED TO

THE MEMBERS OF THE

EDINBURGH

SATURDAY ANGLING CLUB

BY

THEIR SINCERE FRIEND

AND

FIRST PRESIDENT

INTRODUCTORY.

Many attempts have been made to account for the love of angling, which is such a powerful factor in some lives, but all in vain; for this love manifests itself in such varied forms, and upon such a variety of objects, that we are forced to admit that what we term angling is really a composite thing, and cannot be easily defined—appealing, as it does, to so many opposite tastes and emotions.

Thus, one man loves to saunter by silent glens and lonely hills, because he is of a contemplative mind, and, as Burns says—

> "The muse, nae poet ever fand her
> Till by himsel' he learned tae wander
> Adoun some trotting burn's meander."

Another man finds his recreation in the atmosphere of storied scenes. "The battle mound, the Border tower," feed his heart with aspirations and emotions such as nothing else can do. A third has his artistic sense gratified by the picturesque blending of crag and wood, by varied landscape and changing sky.

But, over and above all, there is a constant craving in the heart of man for the restorative, recuperative spirit of nature. As Browning sings—

"O to be in England, now that spring is there!"

We often think that if dwellers in cities could only gratify the craving that comes upon them at certain times, by setting off to the country for a few days of recreation by moor and stream, there would be less of the depression and nerve trouble that is such a sad feature in these pessimistic times. In beginning our rambles, it is necessary that we should get into sympathy with those who are followers of the gentle art; and nothing will do this more effectively than an examination of the impulses that prompt and guide their actions.

With genial Stoddart, who sang the halcyon days of trout-fishing, we invoke the aid of nature in our quest :—

> " Sing, sweet thrushes; forth and sing !
>   Meet the morn upon the lea:
>   Are the emeralds of spring
>   On the angler's trysting-tree ?
>   Tell, sweet thrushes, tell to me,
>   Are there buds on our willow tree ?
>   Buds and birds on the trysting-tree ? "

*   *

*

Two of the following sketches were first printed in the *Weekly Scotsman*, and two in the *Southern Reporter*. For permission to reprint them I sincerely thank the respective editors.

D. F.

CONTENTS.

—◆—

VI.

VII.

VIII.

IX.

X.

XI.

LIST OF ILLUSTRATIONS.

———◆———

RIVERSIDE RAMBLES

OF AN

EDINBURGH ANGLER.

———◆———

I.

AN ANGLER'S FIRST DAY.

THE angler's longing for his favourite pastime usually manifests itself in symptoms of excessive restlessness.

The time of the year when these are most evident is about the beginning of April—glorious, soul-reviving spring! A whiff of west wind has been unexpectedly met with in Princes Street—and from that moment the craving for a glimpse of the country becomes almost intolerable. If you saw such an individual as I have in my mind at present, in the quiet of his own home, you would

A

fail to recognise him as the same staid citizen so
favourably known to the community for his gravity
at kirk and market.

The tokens of a coming change are at first of a
mild nature. There is the usual surreptitious
fingering and fumbling amongst favourite rods and
reels—a dusting of covers and an eager examination of hollow butts. Soon, however, becoming
more bold under their potent inspiration, he dis-
inters the fly-book from its corner in the drawer
sacred to such bric-a-brac, and then, speedily
throwing off all pretence and disguise, he stands
revealed in his true character—a confirmed, irre-
claimable, enthusiastic angler!

When the pipe is not in his mouth a song is;
and in fancy he is away again among the hills,
"where the burnies rin doun to the sea." The
lark is mounting with exulting song to the blue
vault of heaven, the fronds of the reviving
brackens are shooting out verdant sprouts from
their brown parent stems; and down in the
sheltered hollows, facing the south, the darling
flower of spring-time, the bonnie yellow primrose,

is found braving the snell winds in the glens and by the burn side.

Unhappily such mental pictures are difficult to preserve amid the sights and sounds of city life; so the postman's ring, or the tax-collector's knock, are quite sufficient to bring our friend back to earth again, talking prose. But if you would see the angler at his best before the season opens, you must drop in upon him unexpectedly some evening and find him alone.

Mark Antony was not more pathetic over the dagger cuts in Cæsar's robe, than the veteran fisher becomes over favourite flies and their deeds. This fly, now on the retired list, recalls the never-to-be-forgotten tussle with the king of the nutwood pool. That "phantom" brings vividly back the memorable spring-time when he hooked a "kelt" of a roving disposition, which, not content with leading him into the pool waist-deep, succeeded in giving a run for a mile seawards, and then, with two or three mighty lunges, bade our friend farewell!

When the spell of old memories is thus upon

the angler you must listen; it were cruel to deprive
him of the only solace left, for the time when
dreams become realities has not yet come.   In
well meant but decidedly uncertain tones he
occasionally gets vent to his feelings in some such
strain as—

> "I wish I were where Gadie rins,
> At the back o' Benachie."

Another safety-valve for his enthusiasm is found in
reading books or in viewing pictures which treat
of the art he loves so well.   Hence, when the
spring exhibition of the Scottish Academy opens
on the Mound he will be found gloating over such
pictures as "A quiet pool on the Tweed," or "The
burn in spate," or "Caught at last."

These in a measure help the enthusiast to bear
the interval of inactivity and suspense, until, by
and by, after the lapse of some weeks, he is seen
one fine spring morning wending his way to the
Waverley; *en route* for the first day of the season
on the Tweed.

Who can fitly describe in cold and measured

words the throbbing joy of a "first day?" Even
when no longer able to wield rod or wade
water, the veteran angler will thrill with excitement as he recalls the sensations of his early
years. For a while present - day things are forgotten, and in fancy he dwells again with familiar
forms, whose genial presence stamped his early
days as a sportsman with sunlit experiences.

Ruskin, speaking somewhere about the 'Waverley
Novels,' remarks that he had read them again
and again, and always with delight, his only regret
being that he could never hope to experience anew
the peculiar feeling of joy which the anticipation
of their first perusal brought. In like manner the
angler looks upon the novice with feelings that
are almost pathetic, for in the youth before him
he sees himself as he was when all the world
was young — when the sky was cloudless, and
when the keenest bliss he knew in life arose from
the eager anticipation of a long "first day."

A MEMORY.

A first day on the Tweed! recall it not,
　For all around will stale and sombre grow;
A first day on the Tweed! what joy it brought,
　When life was young, and hope's rose tints did glow.

The music of the river worked a spell entrancing
　Around the hearts of lingerers by its shore;
The ripples on the waves in sunlight dancing,
　Memory can ne'er efface till life is o'er.

The thrill of spring's return, 'mid song of glad birds,
　Made pulses throb, and eyes with gladness burn;
The verdant banks, with gowans glinting heavenwards,
　Smiled, as if in joy to herald our return.

Unchanged all seemed to fond imagination
　Since last we trod the gem-bespangled lea;
The cuckoo and the lapwing swelled the diapason
　Which grateful nature sent aloft from field and tree.

We carried in our hearts a song that morning
　Which echoed back from vale and stream and brae;
Would that our lives, fell fortune's buffets scorning,
　Could keep the faith we sang in life's first day!

OVER THE .HILLS TO YARROW

"When first descending from the moorlands,
    I saw the stream of Yarrow glide
Along a bare and open valley,
    The Ettrick Shepherd was my guide."
                              —*Wordsworth*.

II.

OVER THE HILLS TO YARROW.

AFTER a long period of confinement in a city, 'mid carking cares and jading occupations, what can be more healthful to the body or more invigorating to the mind than a short holiday spent among scenes of beauty, and in the pursuit of a sport so absorbing as angling?

The delightful barbarism of breakfasting without your newspaper is as refreshing in its way as is the indifference of the dwellers in the valley to those things which to you seem all-important.

Angling is only a means to an end in the estimation of all true lovers of the "gentle art." You never meet with a keen fisher, but you find him also a passionate lover of nature. The hoary mountain, the silent glen, the lark's song, or the wild bird's note, all create in his breast a rush of feeling too deep for words.

Nowhere in the south is this feeling more nourished than on Tweedside; and it was with the keenest anticipations that, a few years ago, we settled near Peebles for a short holiday. Lovely Tweed! Who can adequately sing its praise? Beautiful alike when issuing from its mountain source, as when, with majestic volume, it rolls past Norham's ancient walls, to find a home in the bosom of the moaning, surging sea.

But not alone for scenery and beauty is the Tweed favourably known. Does not the kingly salmon cleave its waters in search of the rest he, alas! never may enjoy? And as for yellow trout, is not every bend and pool in the river known, not for its fame in Border story, but as the spot where yon memorable basket was got, or as the place where "the largest trout ever seen" made off with your hitherto invincible tackle? There may be streams, particularly in the north, where

you get bigger baskets and bigger fish; but for
all those nameless, indescribable qualities that go
to make up the poetic, artistic side of an angler's
pastime, the Tweed is almost without a rival.

I had been settled in my spring quarters for
some time, when I had the pleasure of a visit
from a young student friend, who intended joining
me in my sport for a few days. It was to him
that I made the proposal one day that we should
start for a long walk next morning over the hills,
by Traquair Kirk and Glenlude, to Yarrow. The
proposal was gladly taken up, and, accordingly,
next morning about four o'clock, when the sun
was struggling to pierce through the veil that hid
his golden splendour, we set out on our long
walk.

> "The lark sent down her revelry;
> The blackbird and the speckled thrush
> 'Good morrow' gave, from brake and bush."

All was bright and promising, and our hearts beat
in unison with the general gladness. The district
we traversed is so familiar in song and story that

it seems almost impertinent to describe our route. Yet, how many are there amongst us who are so engrossed with their studies or their business, that they have no time to become acquainted with scenes of national interest even though these lie at the very door.   There are places of absorbing interest that can be easily reached from town in the course of a Saturday afternoon, and yet there are many intelligent people who know as little about them as we did of the "unexplored territory" on the maps of our school days.

The first place that caught our eye was old Traquair House.   Quaint, moss-grown, and decayed it looks; yet we have seen it gay enough at times, when the last of the old race used on gala days to entertain children from the neighbouring town.   We turned a little off our road in order to see the old iron gate that has never been opened since "the '45." No wonder that it is rusty and ruinous, and that the huge Bradwardine bears on each side of it seem by their fierceness to be resenting such long neglect ! There is now a new gate and lodge, but, though neat enough according

to modern ideas, they seem as much out of keeping
with their surroundings as an oleograph in a German
frame would be in a collection of the old masters.
Crossing the Quair by the old bridge, we could
not deny ourselves the indulgence, so dear to us
in our school days, of lying half over the parapet,
and watching, with the same old feeling of interest
and delight, the glinting movements of the bonnie
trout in the water below. Looking Tweedwards,
we had a fine view of the old house and its out-
lying ground. Traquair House is said to be the
oldest inhabited residence in Scotland; and, if
appearance counts for anything, this statement
may well be true. Gazing at its crow-step gables,
its narrow windows, its stone terrace, and its
"harled" walls, you feel as if it would be the
most natural thing in the world for you to hear
the merry ring of a hunting horn, and were to
see the gate thrown open to allow a gay caval-
cade to pass out to the hawking among the hills
and moors around.

Burton was on the outlook for the "Bush aboon
Traquair," but instead of gratifying his curiosity I

began crooning the picturesque lines of Professor
Shairp on this celebrated spot—lines which Dr
John Brown first gave to the public in his delight-
ful booklet, ' Minchmoor,'—

> "Will ye gang wi' me and fare
> To the bush aboon Traquair?
> Ow'r the high Minchmuir we'll up and awa',
> This bonny simmer noon,
> While the sun shines fair aboon,
> And the licht sklents saftly doon on holm and ba'."

The poet chimes on in this way through many
stanzas as full of music as the murmur of the
Quair itself, until, in the last verse, the key
changes—

> "Now the birks to dust may rot,
> Names o' luvers be forgot,
> Nae lads and lasses there ony mair convene;
> But the blythe lilt o' yon air
> Keeps the bush aboon Traquair,
> And the luve that ance was there, aye fresh and green."

Was it not far better' in such circumstances to
leave Burton with his ideal?

"We have a vision of our own,
Ah, why should we undo it?"

Before reaching Traquair kirk, a road strikes
off on our right, which a finger-post somewhat
vaguely informs us leads "To The Glen," the
estate of Sir Charles Tennant. This place, as we
discovered, is chiefly interesting from the fact that
forty years ago what is now a beautifully wooded
estate was barren moorland. We did not feel
tempted to turn aside, however, but jogged quietly
along, enjoying that most delightful of all experiences—a first glimpse of the country in spring.
How fresh everything looks as it awakes from the
winter's sleep! All nature, animate and inanimate,
seems to be throbbing with returning life; the
very streams are singing in undertones, as if they
were rehearsing their part for the universal chorus
of summer. It may be that what we see is but
the reflex of what we feel, yet who would pause
at such a time to analyse his sensations? Far
wiser is it to give ourselves up to the enjoyment

of the moment, for surely this is what a holiday is meant for.

After passing Traquair kirk the road becomes very steep, and continues so for fully two miles ere it reaches the top of the hill, whence we get our first view of "the dowie dens o' Yarrow." As Burton seemed to have struck up a strong friendship with a shepherd, and was as intent upon the details of sheep-farming as if he were about to settle in New Zealand, I was left to my own thoughts—an arrangement to which I had no objection, as every spot of ground around us brought back memories of the past. From most tourists this part of the road calls forth little enthusiasm. "O the dreary, dreary moorland" would doubtless be their description of it, but far different is it to me at present, for other days and other companions are with me. I hear the sound of merry laughter, and see the glance of bright eyes, which now, alas! will cheer this path no more. There was music in the air in those days such as we never hear now, and even the wild bird's song seemed to have a truer, mellower note.

I was roused from my reverie by Burton shouting, "Why, have you gone to sleep that you have
allowed so many larks to rise without speaking
about them?" "That's because we are going to
the land where larks are as common as sparrows
in a city," I replied. "Did Hogg not write verses
to the skylark?" my friend asked. "Yes, his
'Bird of the wilderness' has much in it that is
both tender and true, but all such verses must
make way for Shelley's beautiful ode—

> "'Hail to thee, blythe spirit!
> Bird thou never wert,
> That from heaven, or near it,
> Pourest thy full heart.
> In profuse strains of unpremeditated art.

> Higher still and higher
> From the earth thou springest,
> Like a cloud of fire
> The blue deep thou wingest,
> And singing still dost soar, and soaring ever singest.'"

"Ah," said Burton, "I must look up Shelley
when I get back to town."

Attention was now drawn to the "Lea Pen," as it appears when you look back upon the road you have travelled, and take your last glimpse of sweet Tweeddale and St Ronan's. My companion's remarks thereon brought to mind some of the conversations we used to share in when a coach ran regularly between Innerleithen and the Lochs. It was no ordinary privilege to travel by this coach, for it was driven by no less a personage than the "Provost" himself. James Lennie was Chief Commissioner of Innerleithen, yet in spite of the giddy height to which he had risen, the Provost had no pride to tarnish his fame. Many a time have we crossed the hill unaccompanied by any other passenger, but this made no difference to our genial friend, as there seemed to be no thoughts of a pecuniary sort in his venture. He loved to drive, and the whole transaction took the form of a hobby; indeed, to all appearance, he was usually happiest when the coach was nearly empty. I don't wonder at my old friend being fond of his occupation—of all the aids to conversation, there is nothing to be compared to travelling by a stage coach. Even martinets soften under such influences, as I can testify from my last coach experience. One of my fellow-passengers was a little military-looking man, who, as we afterwards learned, had seen some service in the West Indies. For a long time he had been very quiet, but he seemed to be intently watching the various features of interest which a changing road ever brings. Suddenly a bird rose from the stream on our right, and with slow, measured beat winged its way down the valley. " What's that ? " eagerly asked our observant friend. " A heron," was the reply, certainly not a *rara avis* in this district. Shortly after a corbie passed us. "What is that ? " was again asked. " A hoodie crow." " Bless my heart," he ejaculated ; " to think that this morning I was in Edinburgh, and now I am in the land of hoodie crows and herons ! "

We were not long in reaching the summit of the hill, and it was with feelings almost of palpitating anxiety that we set our faces steadily

to the front, eager to get the first glimpse of
Yarrow. With the exception of Glenlude farm-
house, which we had just passed, lying in the
glen on the other side of the burn on our right,
there is no habitation near, and the eye has
nothing to rest upon but grassy hills, with here
and there a dark ravine, which is brightened at
other seasons by fern and foxglove.

It is a perfect riever's road, and you almost
expect to meet a drove of stolen cattle at every
turn. A bend in the path, however, soon dis-
closes something much more desirable, for stretch-
ing away beneath us lie the famous haughs of
Yarrow.

Burton at once began—

> "And is this—Yarrow?—*This* the stream
> Of which my fancy cherished,
> So faithfully, a waking dream?"

But I suggested that it were better to wait for
first impressions of our own, for by using the
language of others, beautiful and satisfying though
it be, we dim our receptive, as well as check our

perceptive, powers—shutting ourselves off, as it were, from those potent first influences which leave the most indelible impression on the mind. Burton took my prosing in good part, and replied, "Well, it is quite sufficient reward for my early rising to have entered the atmosphere of enchantment that seems to hover over Yarrow."

And so we kept on our way in silence. Enchantment! That's the word, I thought. Surely years ago Michael Scott laid on the valley a wizard's spell, so that men coming from far should be subdued by it, and, going hence, should be compelled to bring others to the same shrine, that they in turn should be enslaved; until, as the ages rolled on, Yarrow — unknown, peaceful. Yarrow! — should indeed become a very Mecca of the poets! In our mood the silence of the hills was congenial. No sound of busy life was heard, no agricultural activity was seen; and you were fain to fall back, after all, to the utterances of others for fit expression of your feelings. Dr John Brown's beautiful address to the stream comes first to your mind—

"What stream was ever so besung!"

But the well-known lines of Wordsworth fall more glibly from your lips—

"Oh that some minstrel's harp were near,
   To utter notes of gladness;
And chase the stillness from the air,
   That fills my heart with sadness."

But instead of the minstrel's harp, the lark's song was heard suddenly overhead, in strains of welcome to the risen sun.

Mount Benger farm-house was now passed, and we stayed on the summit of the hill for a while, to more fully realise the scene. There is always an intense fascination about the spot where stood the mighty ones now dead. Westminster Abbey can hold us spell-bound, though all the other sights of London clamour ever so imperiously for admiration. Greyfriars' churchyard will draw the stranger to its monuments and tombs with magnetic thrall, though the noise of a great city is heard in ceaseless hum outside its time-stained walls. So now, standing on Mount Benger and gazing on historic scenes, our mind instinctively recalls the personality of those who similarly stood and gazed in bygone years. A vivid picture comes before you of brave men who rode down this path in eager haste, at the sight of the gleaming bale-fire that signalled to them from yonder tower in days of feudal pomp and power. Another scene is pictured in your mind. It is a notable band of patriots, painters, and poets that stands around ; and your heart glows, as you think of their love and admiration for the land and the legends you love so well.

Still another scene. But there is no saying how long this mood might have lasted had not my companion sensibly reminded me of the fact that no amount of poetic rapture would ever fill our basket, so once more jogging along, we soon arrived at the Gordon Arms. This is a charming inn, under the hospitable management of Mr and Mrs Beattie, and, standing as it does where four roads meet, it gives an unlimited choice of fishing in every direction.

We rested here only for a few minutes, and then continued our walk up the valley of the Yarrow to St Mary's Loch and the river Meggat. We were now on classic ground, every mile of which was redolent of Border song and story. On our left flowed the river, gliding under bank and brae with subdued musical murmur; beyond lay Altrive farm, where Hogg lived in the last years of his experience as a farmer, dispensing a generous hospitality which wellnigh impoverished him. Soon we crossed Douglas burn, noted for its many trout, but still more widely famed for its storied tragedy. Rounding a bend in the hill, Dryhope Tower comes in view, where dwelt Mary Scott, the "Flower of Yarrow," and a short distance farther on was seen a dark spot on the hillside, which proved to be the old churchyard where stood in ancient times the far-famed St Mary's Chapel. Our path still lay by the margin of the beautiful loch, so fascinating to poets and travellers; but as we hope some day to speak of St Mary's in detail, it is sufficient to say that I found her then, what I had often considered her before, the queen of lochs for tranquil beauty. Before we reached the river Meggat, which was the stream we hoped to fish, we had to pass a tiny church and a still more tiny post-office at a place called Cappercleuch. There was also a school and a schoolmaster, of whom, as the writers say, "more anon."

Viewing this quiet nook, I could not help saying,—

"If there's peace to be found in the world,
The heart that is humble might seek for it here."

But there was Meggat bridge at last! and flowing beneath were the dark waters from which we were to have an answer to the vexed question—whether there was more pleasure in the pursuit than in the possession of an object?

With the eagerness that only a fisher can understand or be expected to sympathise with, our rods were put together, our flies mounted, and, "o'er a' the ills o' life victorious," we hastened to make our first cast for the season on Meggat. It is a grand sensation having your first fish "on." You begin the capture by making a short cast from the bank where you stand; then you slip down into the water, and wading out a yard or so, still letting out line, you fix your eye upon a deep flow at the far side, where the grassy bank almost touches the water. Casting far and sure, your tail fly just misses the edge of this bank, and with a natural motion alights on the water; there is a moment's suspense, and then the very faintest dimple breaks the surface, then a slight jerk is followed by a strain upon the line, which now goes cutting through the deep water to the music of the reel. Hold up the point of your rod! let there be no straining, no flurry, no impatience to land your fish too soon; but with gentle though firm hand humour his every movement, until you succeed in leading him to where the water runs shallower, when with landing net or steady hand you lay your prize upon the grass.

From the stone bridge over Meggat down to where the stream enters the loch there are some capital

places for a roving fish to lie. Burton was not
aware of this; and so, not long after our start,
I heard him shouting excitedly. Reeling my line
up quickly, I hastened to his assistance, for I
saw, even from a distance, that he had something
"on." The captive was struggling bravely, in spite
of rather cavalier treatment from my friend; for
he, instead of playing the fish cautiously, was
trying to drag it ashore by sheer force. It was
easy to see that it was a fine large trout, for the
water was being lashed into foam by its resist-
ance, and I saw that something would happen
shortly. Something did happen; for, just when I
came forward, the rod unbent and the line
dangled in the air. The gut had snapped!
"Hard lines, Burton," I said. "I wish they
had been harder," said he. How that trout did
grow during the day! At first, a modest "pound-
and-a-half" was set down as its probable weight,
but, whenever it was afterwards mentioned, it
became heavier and heavier, until I had to point
out that every disappointment has its compensa-
tion; for if the giant had been landed it would

have made our basket too heavy for the home-
ward journey !

After this incident, we proceeded up the stream
to the linns above Henderland, where many grand
trout stay all the year round.   The wind was
still rather cold for them rising freely, but we
managed to get one or two plump fellows, in
spite of the earliness of the season.   The trout
of this stream will hold their own for colour or
gameness with the best streams in the south, and
in most of the Selkirk competitions the knowing
anglers take care to be up betimes and away to
Meggat.

I will not dwell upon our further success
this day.   It was really very fair, and in these
degenerate times would even be called good.   The
shadows were lengthening on the hillsides long
before we expected to see them, and as we had
seventeen miles to walk ere we reached the point
we started from in the morning, we had suddenly
to stop.   Indifference to the changing moods of
nature cannot, as a rule, be charged against
anglers.   At anyrate, he would have been a dull

man who failed to be impressed by the picture spread out before him this bright spring afternoon in the uplands of Meggat. Northward, especially, the scene was very striking. Gathering from all points, and deepening as they gathered, were purple-coloured clouds, which, as they hung over Cramalt "Clock," brought singularly near to you the furrowed lines of glistering snow that lay so deep and so hard in the hollows on the higher slopes of the hill.

The return journey was by the same route as we travelled in the morning, but in the light of the setting sun the loch and the hills were seen in additional beauty,—all was loveliness and peace, and the tinkling of the silver rills that trickled down the hillsides seemed a fit accompaniment to the chorus that rose on every hand to heaven from adoring nature.

When we arrived at Traquair the scene had changed, and the moon was shining calmly on the hills and plains, bathing all in silvery light.

The voices of nature, too, were abroad—those strange mysterious sounds and cries that we never hear save at night by the sea waves, or by the river, or on the lonely hillside.

For an addition to our company we had a little sociable stream that panted and gurgled by our side, as if loath to be left behind. He seemed a very twin brother to the one mentioned by Coleridge—

> "That to the sleeping woods,
> All night, singeth a quiet tune."

But on! and soon the glistening waters of Tweed lay on our right, while in the distance a twinkling light from a cottage window spake of an expected arrival, and gave assurance of a hearty welcome home.

FISHING IN ST MARY'S LÓCH

"Oh, loved and lone St Mary's! Thou indeed
Art rich in solemn sad sweet memories!"

—*Annie S. Swan.*

III.

FISHING IN ST MARY'S LOCH.

"The Lake! oh, let not that be made
   A thing of pipes and sluices;
Let something live for beauty's sake,
   Unmixed with baser uses.

Still let it live in fancy's heart
   A haunt for happy fairies,
And make no wretched reservoir
   Of lovely lone St Mary's."
                    —*J. B. S.'s 'Appeal from Yarrow.'*

WE wonder what Scott or Wordsworth would
have said on hearing that some irreverent folk
in Edinburgh were clamouring to get this far-
famed loch converted into a commonplace water-
tank. We know what a modern poet like J. B.
Selkirk has said, and said to good purpose, but
we dare not fancy what the late Professor Veitch

c

would have said if a gang of navvies had been
seen coming up the Yarrow. Interlopers may rest
assured of this, that should infatuation ever lead
them so far astray as to make another attempt to
ruin this locality by destroying its brightest gem,
there are more than "twenty thousand *Border*
men will know the reason why."

In describing the fishing to be had in St Mary's
Loch, it may be well first to give the reader
some idea of its location and surroundings. It
lies in the westmost part of Selkirkshire, about
forty-five miles from Edinburgh. Calmly resting
in a valley hemmed in by imposing hills, it gives
a feeling of tranquillity and restfulness at first
sight which subsequent acquaintance with it, even
when the storm-king rides upon its breast, does
not wholly eradicate.

Roughly speaking, the loch is about three and a
half miles long, from the point where the Yarrow
flows out to the bridge at " Tibbie Shiel's "
cottage. Its broadest part is from the bay below
the kirkyard over to Bowerhope farm, and does
not exceed a mile.

The road from Selkirk to Moffat winds along
its west side, and, excepting at Rodono, there is
an almost total absence of trees. Access to the
loch is easy to be had. You can have the choice
of four routes at least. Thus, train from Edinburgh to Moffat, then take the coach by the Grey
Mare's Tail and Birkhill; or, train to Selkirk, and
travel by coach for nineteen miles up the valley
of the Yarrow, by Bowhill and the "Dowie Dens;"
or go the circular tour, up Ettrick and down
Yarrow, with Bob Scott as prince of guides; or,
train to Innerleithen, and thence by coach *viâ*
Traquair to the head of the loch.

Bob Scott is a character, and has much of the
pawky humour which cheered the soul of good Dean
Ramsay. There are always sayings of Bob's floating
round St Mary's. The latest is this:—A Cockney
tourist was on the coach one day lately, and as
"Watch Law" came into view, he raised his eye-
glass and languidly surveyed some cattle grazing
near the top. "I should think these creatures
would get very little herbage up there," he remarked. Bob answered, as usual, like a flash,

and with delightful irrelevancy, "But, losh, man, look at the view they're gettin'!"

Bob is strong in conundrums. You have not long left the railway station on your trip up the valley before you hear a voice shouting, apropos of nothing in particular, "Why is Scotland the most slave-dealing country in the world?" This voice is Bob's, and this is his way of breaking the ice, before the coach company have been rightly shaken into their places. Various are the attempts made to satisfactorily answer Bob's query; all of them, however, being short of the required one, he at last, in compliance with the request of the lady on the box-seat, solves the mystery thus:—"Because you can buy a *Scotsman* for a penny, and thousands of them are sold every day!"

This essay being hailed as it deserved, the ice soon begins to thaw, and query and rejoinder become general, till Bob remembers his duty as courier, and you hear him begin again:—"This is where the battle of Philiphaugh was focht," etc., etc.

When the late Professor Blackie spent a season at Kirkstead, at the east end of St Mary's Loch, he made the acquaintance of Bob, and greatly enjoyed his quick wit and racy humour. Our popular friend usually has the laugh on his side, but the genial Professor more than once turned the tables upon him. As a mark of esteem the Professor gave Bob the present of a book, on which he had written an inscription in Greek. This mysterious inscription sorely puzzled Bob, and he produced the book on all occasions when he had a passenger whom he thought, from his appearance, might give him a translation of the characters. But it was of no use; and at last, to satisfy his curiosity, as well as that of his friends, he applied to the donor of the book for a translation. The end of their interview must be told in Bob's vernacular:—"' Professor,' I said, 'I wad like t' ken the meenin' o't.' But, losh, man, he turns on me, an' shouts 'What! ye dinna ken Greek? Tak' it t' yer minister, an' if he canna tell 'e, send him t' me!'"

On another occasion the Professor again scored.

The Road Trustees had built a new bridge over Kirkstead Burn, near where it flows into the Loch, at the head of the Yarrow. This bridge was completed just about the end of the coaching season, and one day as the "Flower of Yarrow" came speeding up the glen, with Bob in charge, in all his glory, the Professor was seen standing near the burn with something in his hand. The coach was stopped on a signal from him, and he intimated that he was about to perform the ceremony of opening the new bridge. The "something" in his hand turned out to be a bottle filled with a very suggestive liquid. Gravely sprinkling some of this liquid on the bridge, he poured a further supply into a vessel and handed it up to Bob. Accepting this with thanks, our friend quaffed it expectantly. A curious expression played upon his face for a moment, as he realised he had been hoaxed—it was water from the burn!

The chief tributary of the loch is the river Meggat, famous in the 'Noctes,' but still more famous in the memory of every south country angler. This romantic stream rises in the west, near the source of the Talla, and, after a course of about seven miles, falls into the loch about two miles from the point where the Yarrow flows out. In its short course the Meggat receives no fewer than ten tributaries, some of them streams of no mean order. Winterhope Burn, for example, is larger than the main stream where the junction takes place, while the Cramalt and the Glengaber are burns of considerable volume.

These are all good streams for trout, but we wish some of those people who desire the water for domestic purposes could see them when they are even only slightly flooded. At such a time the sediment imparts a distinct "body" to them, and they bear out what a worthy of the district truly remarked to the writer on one occasion :—" Tak' the water, mon, tak' the water ; it will baith be meat and drink to you when it wins to Edinbro'." Kirkstead Burn is the only other stream which falls into the loch worthy of mention, although the Summerhope, when in flood, is not to be despised.

The Loch of the Lowes lies at the head of St Mary's, and is only separated from it by a narrow isthmus. It is barely a mile long, and is connected to its larger neighbour by a little stream which flows from it directly opposite Hogg's Monument. There can be no doubt that at one time the lochs were one sheet of water, but the *débris* from Crosscleuch Burn has in the course of ages made the division. The same process of silting up may be seen going on at the mouth of the Meggat, and ages hence the angler of that day may find a barrier extending right across the middle of the loch.

For fishing purposes St Mary's is what may be called an "early" loch. Long before the "march brown" has been seen on the Tweed or the Clyde, an imitation of it, in conjunction with the "Greenwell," may be used with deadly effect amongst the finny tribes of this region. We have been told by one of the best fishers of this district that occasionally, in a mild season, he has taken a good basket out of the loch in February. Personally, we have never fished it before the

end of April, at which season it is almost at its best.

Usually there are two kinds of trout in the loch. One is a silvery fish, rather white in the flesh; the other is of a yellow hue, pink in the flesh, and more lively. In the autumn there is a third fish to be got, which, were we fishing the Annan or the Nith, we would call a herling. It runs from four to six ounces in weight, and leaps out of the water several times after it is hooked. It would be interesting to learn to what order this fish really belongs. The local fishers, when appealed to, simply say, "Oh, juist a loch troot;" but as it cuts up a beautiful pink, and the silvery trout of the loch, as we have already said, are white in the flesh, there must be a distinct difference in their classification. Our own idea is that it is a young sea trout, but where it passed its smolt stage is at present a mystery.

In the end of autumn many sea trout and bull trout find their way to the loch, and on to its remotest tributary. They have made the long run of not less than eighty miles from the sea, to deposit their spawn in the shallow gravelly beds of these mountain streams. It would be rash to hazard a guess as to what percentage of them are ever allowed to return to their native element.

Formerly there were few boats on the loch, but at the time of our last visit we counted no fewer than ten, which belong to farms and houses in the neighbourhood. Regarding modes of fishing, we may say that, although there is a certain feeling of luxury in fishing from a boat, with the water lapping at the keel as it quietly drifts across some favourite bay; or, still more, when you sit and allow a "phantom" or an "angel" to troll behind you, while another fellow minds the oars, yet we prefer to fish St Mary's from the shore. This can be done either with or without waders; besides, from frequent experience both by shore and by boat, we conclude the shore fishing to be the most likely to fill the basket. We rather think this was the opinion of both Stewart and Stoddart.

Local tradition has it that there are many large trout in the depths of St Mary's Loch, but they are seldom seen; and the largest ones we can

really authenticate weighed from four up to six
pounds. Such fish are only caught at rare
intervals, and it must be admitted that the average size of the trout here is rather small. Three
to a pound or so, and seven pounds in all, may
be considered a good day's take by any one who
fishes for sport.

One thing that makes a holiday in the vicinity
of St Mary's Loch so enjoyable is the unfailing
courtesy and primitive ways of the people of the
district. Most of them, whether farmers, or shepherds, or gamekeepers, are the representatives of
families who for generations have dwelt there, and
whose names are household words, interwoven as
they are with every incident and tradition of the
place.

Then, again, all honour to the lairds whose
lands lie adjacent to the loch and its tributaries
for the facilities they give the angler when pursuing his favourite pastime. It is often invidious to
mention names, but in this connection the thanks
of every true sportsman should be awarded to the
Duke of Buccleuch, the Earl of Wemyss, Lord

Napier of Ettrick, and the Laird of Rodono. Such action is the more worthy of our appreciation, continuing as it does at a time when, unfortunately, the tendency of others in a like position is towards a selfish exclusiveness.

Surely it is a pleasure in these busy times to know that there still remains a district in our land where, by burn, river, and loch, through many a witchin' glen and many a peaceful vale, the jaded toiler may wander as he wills, till the noise of the city has given place to the hum of Nature's great diapason, and an exquisite peace settles on his soul!

Quoting again from " J. B. S.," we say to all who would ruthlessly lay hands on St Mary's Loch—

> " Oh, touch it not; but let it be
>   As Nature has arrayed it,
>   As softening time has sanctified,
>   And poet's fancy made it.
>   A vale where world-weary feet
>   May come to rest or roam in,
>   Where pilgrim long has found so much,
>   And we have found a home in."

THE POSTMISTRESS OF CAPPER-CLEUCH

"Couthy, kindly, frank and free,
Pawky, helpfu', bauld and slee;
Liked by a' the south countree,
Was Auld Capper Nell."

IV.

THE POSTMISTRESS OF CAPPER-
CLEUCH.

ANOTHER Forest worthy has been taken from us,
and the news that "Auld Nell" is dead will cause
a feeling of sadness to many, both far and near,
whose lot it may have been either to live in the
district or to visit, as a passer-by, the Capper
Post Office. Since the death of Tibbie Shiel, no
one on the loch side was better known than Nell.
Gnarled and browned by the winds that blow o'er
Bowerhope Law, she bore the weight of ninety-
one years with astonishing elasticity and vigour.
In integrity and industry she was a grand type of
her class, and Her Majesty's Postmaster-General
had no worthier servant than she who had charge
of the humble post office at the head of Yarrow.

*

Mrs Ross—better known as Nell—was the widow of
James Ross, a Waterloo veteran, who, after his
discharge from the army, settled at Yarrowfeus
as a district tailor. They did not remain there
very long, and fifty years have passed since they
went up to Capperleuch to keep the gate which
then separated Henderland from Kirkstead farm.
For this humble office they got a free house, and
as they were always willing to oblige by taking
care of parcels from the carrier for the folk who
lived up the glens, they soon became popular in
the district. There was no post office at the Loch
then, and the dwellers among the hills had just
to content themselves with having their letters
brought on from Selkirk or Moffat by the weekly
carrier or a chance passer-by. Sometimes
funeral letters would arrive days after the time
fixed for the interment; and letters from dealers
making an appointment with a farmer to meet
at a certain place would remain basking in the
window of a wayside cottage for days after the
event should have come off. As further showing
the state of the Loch district before the advent of

Nell as postmistress, we may mention an incident told us not long ago by a daughter of Tibbie Shiel. The late Mr Alexander Russel, editor of the *Scotsman*, being, as she said, "a rale guid fisher," was very fond of spending a few days among the trout streams of St Mary's Loch. On one occasion when he was having a holiday here the carrier was told to call at Moffat for his letters. In due time that worthy put in an appearance, and it is easy to picture the sensation he made when, in a tone of amazement, he ex-claimed—"There were mair letters an' papers yonder for ae man than ever I saw in my life; but, faith! I just filled my mooth-pock, an' that's suirely eneuch for onybody." Such incidents led to Nell being installed at the Capper or Copper Cleuch, in full charge of a real post office, where there is a daily dispatch and arrival to and from Selkirk. Besides serving the public well, Nell was a great favourite with tourists, and on coach days her striking head-gear caused many a smile, and got her many a cheer from the passers-by. Indeed, it is difficult to know how "Bob Scott"

D

will get along without her well-known figure to
give point to his stories about "the general post
office round the corner." Nell left for Caddon-
water in April 1893, and so was spared the sight
of the telegraph-posts which have been erected
since, now rearing their gaunt heads along the
loch side. We saw her the day before she left,
and though striving hard to hide her feelings a
the prospect of leaving the spot where she had
spent so many of her days, she was sorely
cast down. And little wonder! under a rugged
exterior there was a heart in full touch with
every memory that clings around the district.
To have seen and spoken with Scott, Hogg,
Wilson, Russel, Chambers, and all the other
famous men who loved St Mary's, was an experience which had left a deep impression upon
our old friend. Excusing her somewhat broken
good-bye, by muttering something about being
"sair troubled wi' a hoarseness th' day," and
with a kindly shake of her hand, the old body
turned sorrowfully away. In cases of sickness,
Nell was considered a "rale skeely body," and,

no doctor being obtainable within many miles' distance, her prescriptions and advice were eagerly sought for. On Sundays she was a picture— clad in decent black, with a large bonnet of fashion fifty years ago. She was seldom absent from the little church which stands on the knoll overlooking the Capper bay. She invariably carried a big Bible in her hand, and on it was laid a neatly folded white pocket - handkerchief, while placed between the leaves was a stalk of the indispensable strong - smelling "speerimint." The last time we saw Nell at church she sat alone in a seat on the right of the pulpit. When the "ladle" was taken round, somehow Nell was missed that day. It is difficult to describe her look of amazement at such an oversight; and no sooner was the service over than she marched up to the "desk," and, with an emphatic click, she deposited her penny on the book-board before the astonished eyes of her worthy friend and neighbour, the pre- centor. Nell took a great interest in the doings of the anglers who came to the district, and could tell of their latest success, or the reverse, with surprising nicety. The deeds of ordinary fishers were passed over by the admission that they were doing "gey weel;" but the common-place doings of her favourites came in for special mention, and reached the summit of commendation when, in answer to a casual enquiry, she was quick to reply that they were catching "sackfu's." Ah, well! peace be to her memory; another link with bygone days is broken. Yet it can · be truly said that Yarrow kirkyard holds none who served their day and generation more faithfully than did Nell of the Capper Cleuch.

LUX IN TENEBRIS.

To A. M.

TEN years have passed since that quiet autumn night
  We climbed the hill together, to the old churchyard :
The loch lay still and lone, dreaming in gloaming light ;
  The massive hills, time's sentinels, stood frowningly on guard.

No sound was in the air, save eerie scream of wild bird,
  As, startled from his heathery nest, he skyward flew ;
No living form was seen, no fitful breezes stirred,
  While deeper and more ominous the mystic shadows grew.

One twinkling light from lonely farm-house smiled,
  Bright token of a warmer glow in hearts within ;
Far in the west the sun was lost, 'mid dark clouds piled,
  Like cliffs of doubt, shrouding the soul in shadows dim.

We spoke of those who said—" Our times were made for
    work ; "
How, " Naught that rested could be heaven sent : "
That " Evil did in poet's contemplation lurk ; "
  " True joy was only found, when strife with victory blent."

Communing thus, we reached God's Acre on the lone hillside,
  Where knights and humble shepherds quietly slumbered :
Visions of Yarrow's Flower, and Douglas' ill-starred bride
  Flashed through our minds, e'en while life's plan we ponder'd.

Far through the haze the loch-born stream did loom,
  And to our ears a plaintive voice seem'd ever calling ;
As if a spirit in the wave bewailed the doom
  Of banishment from lone St Mary's haunts enthralling.

Suddenly, from over lofty Bowerhope hill, all radiant
  The moon burst through the clouds with dazzling gleam ;
Transforming shrouded peaks, which erstwhile had lain dor-
    mant,
  To sentient creatures, clad in silver sheen !

The river caught the impress of the transformation,
  And changed from doleful plaint to strains of hope and joy.
The ruined towers, the farm beneath the dark plantation,
  Like hospices, stood bold and clear, against the sky.

Across the loch a shimmering pathway streamed,
  And rippled to the heather 'neath our feet ;
Flown was the mist ! revealing that, which blindly we had
    deemed
  Lifeless, to be our favourite haunts so sweet !

And thus we learned the truth, that darkness is not blight ;
  That they may do great work who only rest ;
That man, like nature, gains his quest, and takes his posture
    right,
  When patiently he waits for Heaven's own light to radiate
    his breast.

THE SCHOOLMASTER OF CAPPER-CLEUCH

" And still they gazed, and still the wonder grew,
That one small head could carry all he knew.

     .

Lands he could measure, terms and tides presage,
And e'en the story went that he could gauge."
                               —Goldsmith.

V.

THE SCHOOLMASTER OF CAPPER-
CLEUCH.

THE first time we saw Mac. was on a Sunday
morning towards the end of April, about twenty
years ago. We had left the town somewhat tired
and dispirited the day before, and as we sat
looking out of the window of the Gordon, the
scene before us was scarcely fitted to dispel that
mood. A deep mist, which had hung over the
hills all morning, had now merged into an un-
comfortable drizzle, and the east wind was careful
to see that no part of any one compelled to be
out should escape its penetrative power. The
very ducks were huddling disconsolately under a
hedge, and Ned, the collie, only once attempted
to face the drizzle for his morning run up to

Yarrow Bridge ; but the attempt was quite enough, for, ere he had crossed the road, he, with an apologetic wag of his expressive tail, crept back to his warm bed in the stable.

It was at this moment that a man appeared in sight, who walked with a firm, quick step in the face of the gale as it blew up the valley. He seemed somewhat past middle life, and was clad in dark grey homespun. In addition, he had on a large plaid, which was not thrown over his shoulders in the usual way, but was wrapped in a broad fold well round the body. In his hand he carried a large crook, but apparently more for companionship than for support. In a moment he had passed the window, and the whole landscape became once more dreary and lifeless.

This pedestrian was M'Allister of the Capper, teacher, elder, and precentor in the Free Church of Yarrow, now on his way to the forenoon service at Yarrowfeus. The distance he had to walk each Sunday to the Feus and home again was about fifteen miles, and besides this, on each alternate Sunday he was no sooner home than he had to lead the singing at the Loch Church. We were fortunate in having the pleasure of becoming intimate with Mac., and for twenty years had increasing opportunities of knowing his sterling worth. At the time of his death he had been for the long period of forty-three years the trusted friend of all in the district. To visitors his courtesy was unfailing, and his local knowledge was invaluable, for no better fisher ever cast a line on St Mary's Loch. His enthusiasm for, and sympathy with, all sport and sportsmen was as keen in old age as ever it was in his youth; and, what is not so common, his love for the scenery of the district never wavered for a moment. Many a time, when walking by the loch or the river, he would stop with an exclamation of admiration, and draw your attention to some aspect of the scenery, as if he had never seen it before. Mac. was, in the language of the district, wonderfully "yauld,"—*i.e.*, supple or agile. He was also of a very sociable disposition, as was shown by the way in which he would accompany a friend over moor or mountain to help either in fishing or in shooting. Panniers of game were seemingly just as easy for Mac. to carry as panniers of trout. We recall an incident which shows his character in daily life. One evening we were returning from the east end of the loch, and had arrived at the "Ged lake," a small estuary of St Mary's, when we were hailed by Mac. and advised to try a cast in the Ged. While doing this, the bob fly caught in a weed near the edge, and quite beyond a projecting dyke which jutted out into the water. In a moment our friend's foot was on the wall, and, with the agility of a youth, he was over and had detached the fly and was back again ere you had time to realise the situation.

More than once Mac. was sent as a representative elder to the Free Church General Assembly. The last occasion on which we saw him there was on the morning of a "Declaratory Act" day. The house was very full, but the eye was at once caught by a figure in grey tweed sitting on the front seat at the right hand of the Moderator. This seat is usually reserved by courtesy for ex-

Moderators or Fathers of some prominence, but, all unconcernedly amid the black coats, there sat Mac. quite at home. "Yon's the very seat for me," he said subsequently; "I fixed on it the first time ever I was there." Well, in view of his services to the Church, as already mentioned, a worthier man could not have occupied it.

Mac. now sleeps in the lonely churchyard of St Mary's Chapel, which overlooks the loch he loved so well; and the spot is made all the more dear to many of us because such a true heart rests there.

A DAY ON LOCH LEVEN.

"" The hill of Benarty stands bold to the sky,
And down in the valley Loch Leven doth lie.
The isle like a gem on its bosom is gleaming,
While high o'er the castle the wild gull is screaming."
—*Old Song.*

VI.

A DAY ON LOCH LEVEN.

It is twelve years since I had my first experience of Loch Leven. Many a time had I been told that no man could be called a fisher who had not filled his creel on that famous loch; but of this I was doubtful, for I had also been told that no man could count himself a fisher unless he had killed a salmon, and I had seen both done by mere duffers.

One day in July as I was walking along Princes Street, I met my old friend MacLeod, smiling all over. I soon found out the cause, as he showed me a "wire" from the "Captain," saying that a boat could be had on Saturday, and that the fishing was good. Who, of all the followers of Izaak, could resist the temptation of a place in the boat with such an enthusiastic companion as Mac.?

E

Certainly not the present writer. So, Saturday morning found us at the Waverley, investing in a third return for Loch Leven.

In the days before the Forth Bridge so improved matters, it used to be a " lang, dreich road " to Loch Leven by Granton and Burntisland. Still, on this occasion I could not complain, for I was fortunate in getting into a friendly talk with a Fife fisherman, returning from the East Coast herring fishing. He seemed to look upon amateur fishers with something of the same kind of toleration and condescension that the regular soldiers used to show to Volunteers away back about '59; but I was only too anxious to profit by his experience. " You should use strange baits," said he; "strange baits aye raises fishes' curiosity." " Now," he continued, " if I was to gae and fish Loch Leven, I would hae naething to dae wi' your shop flees; I wad try a screed o' a whiting's breest; it shines, ye see; it shines!" I ventured to mention that it was not mackerel but trout I was after, but his rejoinder had always the same refrain — " Try strange baits; fishes is curious!"

This was certainly past denying; so, by way of changing the subject, I expressed my admiration for the conduct of the crews of a fishing fleet in a recent disaster. To this my friend replied—" But a man will ne'er be drooned till his time comes, and aince that comes naething will save him !" My fatalistic companion had to leave me at Burntisland ; but reverting once more to our crack about fishing, his parting words were—" Aye try strange baits; fishes is curious."

Fife trains are always unwilling to part with you; but, after frequent delays, we were at last put down at Loch Leven. The morning was calm and bright, with just enough of wind to ripple the water most invitingly. Little time was lost in starting from the pier, for our boat and two men to manage her were all ready when we arrived. The boat is usually in charge of one of the men who is called the " skipper," and the individual who filled this post for us was a Dutch-built, elderly man, whose gravity was most impressive. No captain of a three-decker could have taken his responsibilities more seriously than he did.

Being a stranger to the ways of the loch, had I been alone I would have required to put myself into the hands of the boatmen, for them to do with me what they pleased; but, fortunately, MacLeod was an old frequenter of Loch Leven, so he directed the boatmen to row out far beyond the island, that we might have a good long drift for the first one.

While we were being taken there, Mac. put out his trolling rod with an angel minnow in tow, and we were scarcely five hundred yards from the pier when whir-r-r went the reel, and a lovely trout leaped and gleamed in the sunlight; but it was in vain that he dived and leaped and struggled, for he was soon brought to the net, and so number one fell to my friend's rod. Meanwhile, we were gradually approaching that part of the loch where we intended beginning our drift, and it was with no little concern that I observed that the wind, which had been all that the most fastidious fisher could have wished, was now falling away. The sun also had become very strong, and was casting a harsh glare upon the water. To a remark of mine that there was still a good swell upon the loch, the skipper answered, "Ah, but there's ower muckle hale water." He meant that the waves, instead of having a nice shimmery, broken crest, were rising and falling with an oily undulating motion.

However, it takes a lot to damp the ardour of a fisher, so with a cast comprising a "professor," a "woodcock," a "bustard," and a "Zulu," I eagerly took my place in the stern—Mac. being at the bow—and began operations. At first, a novice in boat fishing finds that he cannot by any means give undivided attention to his flies; he is more concerned in finding his sea legs. But this distraction is soon lessened, and in a little while he falls into a way of casting which is regulated by the motion of the boat.

For more than an hour we kept casting, one time drowning, at another skimming our flies, but all to no purpose. There seemed to be an in-tangible, incomprehensible "something" in the air. The skipper from time to time prompted me with such hints as "Throw in the hough o' the

wave," or "Aye keep your flees on the water"—
practical advice of the most valuable description.
Many a time since then, on many a loch and
river, when I was disposed to lose heart or grow
weary, there has come to my mind, like the refrain
of an old song, the skipper's words—"Aye keep
your flees on the water."

The forenoon was almost blank; no wind, no
cloud, no fish!　Shortly after two o'clock, however, dark clouds began to creep over Benarty,
and soon the sound of thunder broke upon our ear.
"It's gaun to be an awfu' storm," said the skipper.
"Let's row ashore," said his mate.　"Not a
bit of you," said Mac.; "I saw a fish rise this
very minute."　And rise they truly did, now here,
now there, until the loch was dimpled all over
with them.　"Bring the net," was soon a frequent
cry, and more than once, each of us had a fish
on at the same time.　"This beats a'," said the
skipper; "I aye thocht they didna tak' in thunner."
So did we, but this afternoon's experience com-
pletely dispelled that notion.

Frequently since then, we have found that

previous to the storm bursting the fish lie at the bottom, but no sooner does the air seem to clear and the rain begin to fall than they become active, and are ready to take anything. On the occasion I am describing the storm lasted for more than an hour, and during that time we caught twenty-five trout, weighing fully twenty pounds.

It was a lovely evening as we pulled to the pier. The loch reflected an almost unrivalled blue sky, the fields also were fresh and smiling after the rain, and in the north two peaks of the Ochils were spanned by a gorgeous rainbow. " Weel," said our second boatman, who seemed a bit of a philosopher, " had ye seen that in a picter ye wadna hae believed it ! "

"AYE KEEP YOUR FLEES ON THE WATER."

(Loch Leven Boatman's Advice.)

On the river of life when the current runs low,
  And the waves 'mong the pebbles creep on with dull clatter,
Be it ours ever faithful, 'mid gladness or woe,
  To ply still our task, with our flees on the water.

When the sun's in the sky, and the winds gently blow,
  And the flowers of prosperity all gloom seem to scatter,
May humility lead us, with step modest and slow,
  To where best we can kindly cast our flees on the water.

When the water's in trim, and our hope of success
  Gleams bright as a rainbow, the project to flatter—
'Tis most trying for adepts to frankly confess
  That a duffer has won by bait-fishing the water.

Should the dark clouds appear, and the sky be o'ercast,
  And the wind of adversity our hopes rudely shatter,
No bield will we seek till the storm be blown past,
  But, manfully striving, keep our flees on the water.

DARK LOCH SKENE

"Yet him whose heart is ill at ease
　Such peaceful solitudes displease:
He loves to drown his bosom's jar
　Amid the elemental war;
And my black palmer's choice had been
　Some ruder and more savage scene,
Like that which frowns round dark Loch Skene."

VII.

DARK LOCH SKENE.

"There eagles scream from isle to shore;
Down all the rocks the torrents roar;
O'er the black waves incessant driven,
Dark mists infect the summer heaven;
Through the rude barriers of the lake,
Away its hurrying waters break,
Faster and whiter dash and curl,
Till down yon dark abyss they hurl."
　　　　　　　　　—Scott.

HE who visits Loch Skene solely for the sake of its trout will find that he has made a great mistake. True, they are little beauties, but the weather in the heights where the loch lies is so uncertain that you rarely find a day that can in every particular be considered favourable for sport. If it is fair while you are there, the probability

is that you have arrived all bedraggled, after a
toilsome climb from Birkhill. If, on the other
hand, you have got there with something like a
tolerable measure of comfort, you no sooner put up
your rod, and mount your most killing flies, than
you perceive that the mist that has been playing
at hide-and-seek near the summit of the White
Coomb has begun to creep down to the base; and
up the Winterhope Burn there comes the sound of
a rising storm. In such circumstances the surface
of the loch changes from a gentle ripple to agitated
white-capped waves, which foam and break on the
submerged rocks, as well as on the piled-up
boulders that surround the shore. All this is
cheerless, and even though you give a shout to
relieve the tension of your feelings, you only inten-
sify the solitude, for from the islet just beyond the
bay on your left there rises a solitary heron, which,
with lazy wing, manages to move to the peninsula
a few yards away. But by your shout you have
succeeded in disturbing the slumbering echoes, and
from the crater-like hills opposite there come
moaning and protesting sounds, such as might

issue from the cave where dwell the genii of the loch. If these fitful moods be characteristic of the place, why do anglers in the south of Scotland never rest till they have made a pilgrimage to Loch Skene? Well, although we have been there in all its moods, and have got more thoroughly " wat " amongst the peat-hags than ever before or since, we cannot venture to answer that. If we could, we would be in a fair way to account for some of the mysteries of life, and be on the verge of getting a glimpse of those things in heaven and earth which have hitherto eluded the compass of our philosophy. It was with none of these thoughts in our mind that T. and I left the bonnie haughs of Henderland on our way to the loch one day towards the end of August two years ago. To get there, our course lay south-westward, by the margin of St Mary's Loch, and that of the Loch of the Lowes; then up the glen where flows the Little Yarrow, and finally, on to the summit called Birkhill — the dividing line between Selkirk and Dumfries.

Here we left the road, and stepping on to the

moor on our right we made for a half-defined path which is seen gradually rising towards the towering hills in the west. Before ascending the hill we did what no true lover of Scottish character should fail to do—we took the liberty of making a call at Birkhill Cottage. A welcome from Mrs Brown there is like a cordial to a jaded spirit, while a crack with her worthy husband is an education.

Remember that this is no mere inn, but the cottage where dwells the shepherd, who, for many years, has looked after the pastures that extend from his door to the hill beyond the cliffs which overhang the famous fall of the "Grey Mare's Tail." Many a weary traveller has had cause to be thankful that there was such a hospice as Birkhill Cottage, and such kind hearts within it. And yet this cottage, like the hills that surround it, has seen as much of cloud as of sunshine, for sitting by the fireside after everything has been done up for the night, you may hear, amongst other things, of a tragic occurrence which happened to a young relative of the family.

One day in early winter, some forty years ago, this young shepherd had to send his dog after some sheep that had got lodged in the ribbed slope of the hill which rises almost perpendicularly from a ravine about a quarter-of-a-mile below the cottage. The dog lost heart, and the youth, with that regard for his dumb friend so characteristic of shepherds in general, ventured some distance along the hillside to encourage the dog to further effort, but unfortunately he missed his footing, and fell headlong down the hill into the bed of the stream below. And so another cairn was added to the many that stand on the slopes of our southland hills, bearing witness to the courage and the devotion to duty of the shepherd race.

Mindful of many a hearty welcome in past times, we duly paid our respects at Birkhill on the morning I am describing. This we did none the less readily that a dense mist had for the last mile or two been making us somewhat disagreeably aware of its presence. We were fortunate in finding both the shepherd and his wife at home, and after some talk about mutual friends and ac-

quaintances, James, with that weather knowledge
that comes of long experience, strongly advised us
not to make the trip to Loch Skene that day.
" Ye are better here than there, for mony that ken
the road weel wad miss it on a day like this."

There were many inducements, besides this
friendly warning, inclining us to stay; but then,
what fisher has the moral courage to turn back in
his project, and risk ridicule?   Better, far better
to expose himself to the elements, though the
only thing caught that day be catarrh and rheu-
matism ! With a cheerie good-bye, therefore, and
a promise to look in on our return, we began the
ascent to Loch Skene.

The mist by this time hung heavy all around
us, and the wind was rising and coming in fitful
gusts up the valley.   Our hope was that the rain
would fall so heavily as to clear away the mist and
enable us to see for at least a reasonable distance
in front. But we were disappointed. Denser still
came down the mist, and splash! slush! slush!
we went on through oozing peat-hags and swollen
sheep drains. Every runlet had now become a

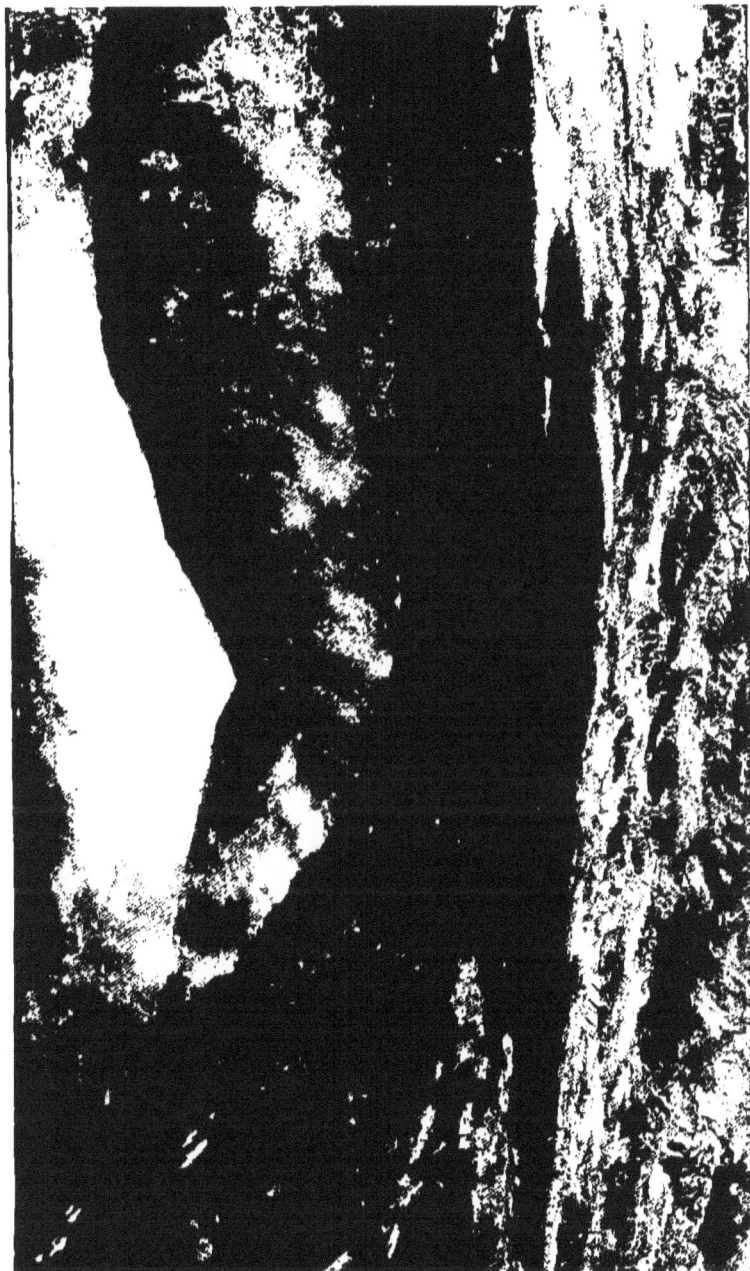

torrent, and in leaping from hag to hag we sometimes leaped short, and sank almost to the depth
of a foot in peat mould. Through all this,
nature was strangely silent; an occasional "gluck,
gluck," from a startled blackcock, or the weird
scream of the curlew, were the only sounds, at
long intervals. Truly, cold and dreary is the
landscape when not illumined by the glorious sun!
We feared we should have lost our way, but somehow our bump of locality was too strong for that;
yet we must have deviated from the course a
good bit, for it was fully two hours after we
had left Birkhill before we heard the sound
of the waves breaking on the shore round Loch
Skene.

Now that we had reached our destination it
became doubtful if we would be able to fish after
all. Our hands were stiff and benumbed by the
cold and the rain, and the wind was so gusty
that every now and then we could see entire
sheets of spray being lifted from the loch. Still,
we must have a trout to show that we really
had been there; so after some difficulty our rods

F

were put up, and our casts selected. Since then I have always found bright flies, such as the "professor" or the "pheasant wing," suit the dark waters of this loch; and on this occasion these fully maintained their reputation; for, after fishing not more than two or three minutes, I was fortunate enough to raise and land a nice trout of about six ounces. Meantime, T. was working his way round by the base of the White Coomb, and an occasional whistle across the loch let me know that he also was not without some token of success. But it was chilly work at the best, and our dripping garments and frequently entangled flies would have given scoffers a glorious opportunity to sneer at what we called "sport." Still, brother fishers will admit that our purpose had been accomplished under difficulties of no ordinary kind, and what more does the most ambitious desire?

After fishing for about three hours we counted up our spoils, and found them to reach the somewhat meagre total of twenty trout, averaging about a quarter-of-a-pound each.

The return to Birkhill was a comparatively easy

matter, although the mist was as dense as ever. We had intended to follow the burn that flows from the loch, and which, joining with a little stream that flows from the west side of the high hill I have twice referred to, makes, at a distance of little more than a mile farther down, the picturesque fall of the " Grey Mare's Tail." But to attempt descending the slopes near the fall on such a day as this would have been sheer madness; so we returned by our morning's route. When we reached the shepherd's house our worthy friends stared at us as if they had seen a warlock. "Oo never thocht ye wad be back this wey again," said James; "when folk loss theirsels on that hill, oo aye ken that they wander doun the Wintrup burn."

But the scones and the tea and etceteras that shortly thereafter disappeared from the table proved that we were no spirits, but mortals of a decidedly material order. Good-bye soon followed, and after a walk of seven miles, we found ourselves snugly seated at "oor ain fireside" in bonnie Henderland. Such is the fascination of an outing of this sort that we are already planning for another day at dark Loch Skene!

         *   *

I have been twice at the loch since the day on which the events referred to took place. It might not have been worth while saying so, were it not that I desire to acknowledge how much anglers are indebted to Mr Smith of Craigielands, near Moffat, who has in the most public-spirited manner introduced many thousands of young Loch Leven trout to Loch Skene at his own expense. On one of the days I was there lately I had splendid sport: many of the trout weighed nearly three-quarters of a pound, and though more bronzed in colour, by reason of the dark waters, they showed all the characteristics of the Loch Leven trout.

ROUND THE LAMP AT THE GORDON ARMS

"There stood a simple home, where swells
The meady sward to moory fells;
A rural dwelling, thatched and warm,
Such as might suit the upland farm."

—*Hogg*.

VIII.

ROUND THE LAMP AT THE GORDON ARMS.

MANY a happy night has the middle room in the Gordon Arms seen. The wind from the east might moan past the window in the darkness of a night in early spring, or, equally mournfully, the wind from the west might sigh down the Yarrow when the evening twilight was deepening in pensive autumn; but at all seasons, and after days of all sorts of luck, warm hearts were to be found gathered round the red lamp there, and song and story shut out all cares and thoughts of town. We have looked at the forces clustering round these memories from all sides, and are convinced that our moral fibre got as much strengthening from the *camaraderie* of our evenings there as our physical fibre got from the glorious ozone of the lake and the hills.

We were speaking one night of the lovers of the district we had met at the Gordon. They proved to be almost innumerable, and came from every class and rank of life. Poets, artists, doctors, ministers, teachers, merchants, farmers, all had in turn been under the spell of Yarrow; and in many instances they had left their testimony of love and gratitude in song and verse as tributes to the witchery of the district. Happily, they are not all gone from us, though many have become but pleasant memories. We still have J. B. Selkirk, whose

"September, and the sun was low,"

is as sweet a poem as ever Yarrow inspired. Then we spake of Professor Veitch, the historian of Border poetry, and who was no mean exponent, in his own writings, of the moods of her scenes and traditions. The next day we heard that he also had been taken from the land he so warmly

loved. The following verses are the outcome of
our feelings of regret for his loss.

JOHN VEITCH—IN MEMORIAM.

(Born, 24th October 1829; died, 3d September 1894.)

A song of joy, raised o'er the ripening grain,
  The grateful husbandman doth gladly cheer;
But sound of sighing wind and sobbing rain
  More fittingly attunes the mourner's ear.

A moan of grief comes from Tweed's darkened flood,
  Which sympathetic Nature bears along;
And strath and hill, in sombre, pensive mood,
  Mourn one who changed their fitful lights to song.

Why tarries Yarrow 'mong her ruined towers,
  When spirits from the dowie dens allure her on?
Why chafes the pent-up Ettrick in her birchen bowers?
  And Meggat stream flow dark, with ceaseless moan?

The poet of fair Tweeddale sings no more!
  And hill and glen still quiver with the smart;
Nor crag, nor hill, nor legendary lore
  Shall quicken more his warm, responsive heart.

The love of Nature, which, through strife and din
  Of throbbing academic life, still held him true,

Shone e'er resplendent, as a light within
　Refines the soul, and envy's darts subdue.

Yet shall his spirit pass the quenchless torch along
　To kindred souls, by mountain, stream, and lea,
Until a nobler light hath on them shone,
　Illimitable as joy and dule on life's mysterious sea.

FISHING INCIDENTS.

Fishers' stories are proverbially taken *cum grano salis.* Yet there are few who follow the gentle art who are not able to recall incidents from their own experience, or that of others, which, though needing the aforesaid seasoning, are none the less, as the books of our boyhood used to put it, "founded on fact."

Apropos of the question, Eels *v.* trout. We remember, one afternoon, taking a cast on a pool in Glengaber burn. The water was very clear; and immediately on the fly alighting, a trout rose, but at the same moment a dark object seemed to rise from the bottom of the pool; and ere the trout could seize our fly, it was itself seized by a large

eel. I called to the brother who was accompany-
ing me, and we both distinctly saw the miscreant
swaying to and fro in the pool with a three-ounce
trout in its mouth. The latter had been seized
across the body, so that both tail and head were
projecting from the mouth of the eel on either side.
In this position it remained as long as we could
see, for the captor worked itself under a large rock,
there, no doubt, to devour troutie at leisure.

*   *   *

The voracity of pike is often brought under the
fisher's notice, even when he is not in quest of
them. Once when fishing in St Mary's Loch,
I hooked a trout of a somewhat lively turn.
It plunged about a good deal, and after one of
its headers, I was surprised to feel a great
increase of resisting force, and suddenly the top
piece of my rod began to bend in an alarm-
ing manner. I fancied that I had quite under-
estimated the size of my fish—not a usual fault
of anglers, certainly—but the state of matters
soon became evident when the back fin of a

large pike began to show above the water. I
could only hold on, and, being on the shore,
gradually step backwards. With that tenacious
grip well known to pike fishers, my rival held on
to the trout, and at the same time unconsciously got
himself worked towards the land on the incoming
wave. Naturally elated at the prospect of a double
capture, I handled the rod very cautiously; and,
just when I expected pike and trout together should
have been landed, the former, finding himself
in shallow water, relaxed his grip. The trout was
easily landed, but almost bitten through by the
teeth of his savage foe.

*   *   *

One evening in the same season that the last
mentioned incident occurred, I was fishing at
" Cape Horn" on the south side of the loch, when
I hooked what seemed to be a large trout. He
promised a stiff fight; but judge of my surprise
when he began to swim towards me of his
own accord! On nearing the shore, I got a
glimpse of red fins, and at once saw that a

perch had taken my fly. He proved a very tame capture, although weighing nearly a pound., Surely instances of perch taking an artificial fly are rare.

*   *   *

There is no accounting for the humours of fish. I remember an incident of two fishers having their first cast for the season on the Meggat. They had "fleed her up, and mennanded her doun," but all to no purpose. At last, when they arrived at the pool near the wooden bridge, one of them produced a large moth-eaten salmon fly, and exclaimed that he might "as well make a fool of them as no." This curiosity had no sooner touched the water, than a large fish rose and seized it. The struggle was long, and for a time doubtful; but by-and-by the fish got into shallow water, where it was an easy matter for the angler who was free to get behind him and act in the capacity of a landing-net. The capture proved to be a sea-trout of nine pounds.

*   *   *

A "last cast" is not a bad institution. One spring season, when fishing St Mary's Loch in company with my esteemed friend, the late Mr John Rhind, A.R.S.A., we had naturally got separated—he to the south side, while I worked westward. In the afternoon, when the trap was brought up for our return, the driver remarked, "I don't think Mr Rhind has done much." "Do you think not?" I remarked. "Ay; he was sitting on the bank o' the loch smokin' when I came up, and he said there was naething daein'."

When we came in sight of the east end of the loch, Mr R. was seen wading ashore, preparing to meet us. On handing up his creel, I was surprised to see the tails of two large fish projecting from it. These turned out to belong to two sea-trout, weighing respectively three-and-a-half and two-and-a-quarter pounds. The story of their capture was simply told. It was quite true that little had been doing all day up to the time for the trap coming, but after it had passed, Mr R. thought he might as well try a cast until it returned, giving an interval of half-an-hour or so. He

accordingly tied on a large "red spider," and wading
into the loch as far as he could with safety, he
threw a long line into the deep water; immediately
the larger of the two fish rose, and was hooked at
once. After a good deal of play, he was eventually landed, by the aid of a heavy wave that was
rolling on to the beach. Once more wading in
about the same place, Mr R. rose and hooked
number two, which also was soon encreeled. It is
hard to know what further captures might have been
made had we not appeared on the scene. However,
the last half-hour fully made up for the short-
comings of the previous hours.

*   *   *

A good wave shorewards is the best landing-net
I know of. I have often been struck with the
difference of time taken to land trout in a river compared with the time taken to land fish of the same size
in a loch. In the spring of 1894 it took me over
twenty minutes to land a four-pound sea trout from
the Yarrow; while at the same season of the year in
1891 I landed a yellow trout of the same weight

from St Mary's Loch in five or six minutes. In the
latter instance I gradually stepped backwards, and
a strong east wind almost did the rest. They were
both in prime condition.

*   *   *

A long holiday among the lochs and the rivers
is grand beyond expression, but in its way I know
few pleasures to compare with that of an escape
from town just for a day at a busy time in mid-
summer. The delight of catching the last train
from town on a Friday night, and your drive, or,
better still, your walk in the cool of the evening
to the inn where you put up all night, is full of
elements of the most exhilarating kind. Who can
ever forget the scent of the sweet - brier in a
dewy summer night, or be calm as he recalls the
beauty of the wild roses by the roadside, or that
of the hawthorn blossom and the verdant mosses
by glen and burn? And then your welcome at
the inn or the farm - house where you pass the
night, your hasty run over to the river to see
how it promises for the morrow, and your rest-

lessness and general impatience for the early
dawn !

That the expected sport does not always come off
the following incident will show :—

A COMPETITION EPISODE.

Loud chimed the clock at Gordon Arms,
  Ae sweet mid-summer morning ;
But Jack and chum lay snug in bed,
  Unheedful of its warning.

Late, late at e'en the nicht before,
  From town they baith cam' rushing ;
Glad to escape the city's roar,
  And ha'e a grand day's fishing.

But noo the sun up Yarrow vale
  Glints brichtly through their window ;
Yet who recks sun or stormy gale
  When senses are in limbo ?

" Up, up, my lads, the loch's in trim,
  A ripple's on the river ;   ·
The trouts are loupin' 'neath the linn,
  The burns wi' rises quiver ! "

" But, oh ! how weak are men's resolves,
  Their projects ill to keep ! "

G

Chum up, and off; Jack looks his watch,
    Yawns thrice, and falls asleep!

Lo! quick upon his sleep-swelled brain
    Queen Mab plays mirthful pranks;
For trout and salmon, micht and main,
    Come thronging to the banks.

They fecht to get his bait, they swarm
    In hundreds round his flee;
His creel is brimful; even his rod
    Stands sair in jeopardy.

Salmon in sackfu's line the stream,
    Trouts by the hundred dizzen
Are hook'd and landed—in his dream!—
    Till high the sun has risen.

" What's that?"—A tap comes to the door,
    Jack jumps wi' mighty clatter;
" Please, sir, they thocht ye were na' gaun,
    An' they're lang syne on the water!"

              ✳   ✳   ✳

The effect of colour upon trout has never been
satisfactorily ascertained. That fish have prefer-
ences for certain colours at given seasons is

beyond doubt. It may be that the natural fly is a bright-coloured one, and hence the preference.

Professional fishers have a great contempt for what they call "shop flees," but, for all that, the fish sometimes act as if "there was a method in their madness." Most fishers will recall experiences with singular flies that had been tried as a last resource. For a long time I carried a No. 1 fly in my book that I rather looked upon as a showcase article. It was adorned with a green body and pale brown wings. One day when Douglas Burn was running pretty full, the temptation to leave the Yarrow and strike up by Blackhouse was too great; so in less than three hours I found that I was nearing the Tower—two miles up —but without that weight on my back which the appearance of the water had led me to expect. There are several long pool-like stretches of water about this part of the burn, and as the breeze was blowing upwards, I felt quite disappointed at my non-success. Having to open my book for some purpose, my eye caught the fancy-coloured fly, and thinking that surely now was the time for an experiment, I tied it on as the tail fly. Beginning at the foot of a long pool, I cast the three flies gently upwards: immediately there was a rise, and soon I hooked a nice yellow trout on my new lure. Another cast had the same result, and on through the pool I waded, until, while landing number sixteen on the same fly, a voice said, "I can stand this nae langer; what are ye fishin' wi'?" The questioner turned out to be a shepherd who had been watching me for some time, while I was so absorbed in the sport that I had never seen him!

This good fortune attended me all afternoon, until, unluckily, my killing fly had become "necked," and so, striking somewhat strongly at a good fish, I lost both trout and fly. I was really sorry to lose this curiosity, as I meant to have several made to his pattern; but, like many more things in life, regret came too late.

*   *   *

When fishing with a friend on Loch Leven one evening, he hooked a very large trout—"a fish," he called it; and as he was a tried salmon-fisher, his designation meant something beyond the common. The incident was so exciting that I wound up my line and stopped casting, that undivided attention might be given to the play of the "four-pounder," as the boatman called it.

" Take care," I said; " you're giving too much line." " Not a bit of it! see how his fin cuts through the water! Why, this beats salmon-fishing any day." But my friend's triumph was short-lived; for, giving plenty of line, as he said, there was a strange whirr, and, lo! the end of a good waterproof line, of fifty yards at least, went slipping through the rings of the rod. On putting on the line, he had been guilty of the mistake of forgetting to tie a knot after passing the end through the hole in the centre bar of the reel. For a little we could see the dry line lying on the surface of the water, and the boatmen followed after it with a will, but it gradually got wet through, and fish and flies and fifty yards of line were lost to him for ever.

* * *

In speaking of the Loch of the Lowes and its
perch-fishing, nothing has surprised me more than
the evidence we have of the innumerable quantities
of these fish that haunt its waters.   To my own
knowledge, young fishers who have been fortunate
enough to come upon a shoal of perch in a taking
mood have been literally sated by the numbers
willing to be caught.

One day last August three little boys left
Henderland late in the afternoon to fish for perch
at the Lowes.   They were anxious to try the
virtues of nice little new rods, and their bait bags
were duly replenished with fascinating wrigglers.
The first bay they tried yielded no sport, but on
moving a little more to the east there was a
shout from the smallest boy of the three "that
he'd got a pike on!"   This proved to be a perch of
half-a-pound.   Boy-like, they all went to fish at the
same spot, and great was their delight when each
in turn pulled out a fish.   This went on until
the fifteen-pound basket, which one of the lads
had, was packed to the lid with really pretty fish.
Their next plan was to string their captures

through the gills on to some fishing cord until there was no room for more.

By this time the shadows were lengthening on the hill sides, and, what was more felt by them, their bait was done; so they began to think of stopping. Not so the fish, for they seemed as eager to be caught as ever. At home we were beginning to be anxious, so one of us set out to hurry them up, and he met the fishers about two miles from the loch, "stachering" along under their several loads. 'Twere vain to attempt to describe their excitement at the capture of about thirty pounds of fish, and we may be sure that their sport on this occasion will never be forgotten as long as they live.

This experience was even outdone by that of two sons of Mr Satterthwaite of Lancaster, who were fishing in the loch the year before.

*　　*　　*

Pain in trout is a mystery, and I am always glad to meet with any one who in the most positive manner asserts that fish " feel " very little discomfort when struggling to be free from the hook. Most fishers can tell of cases in their own experience where fish acted as if they rather liked to be hooked than otherwise. More than once I have caught fish which sported sharp hooks and a length of gut in their jaws; and the cases are common where, after I had lost a fly through sharp striking, in a minute after the same trout rose, was hooked, and landed with the first fly still sticking in his mouth. Two years ago I was fishing up the Armit, and lost a bait hook with about eighteen inches of gut, by striking too quickly, before the gut was softened. On coming down the river side four hours later, I suddenly recalled the fact that it was just at this place I had the misadventure in the morning, so I thought it worth while to try again. I did so, and instantly my lure was seized; and, after a little play, there was a nice half-pound trout landed with my lost hook firmly fixed in his throat, and the gut projecting from the mouth.

※ ， ※ ※

Mist on the hills is fatal to loch fishing. When
the clouds have settled upon Capper Law and
Bowerhope, the angler had better make for the
Meggat with all speed, for few will be the trout
caught that day on St Mary's until the mist lifts.
We remember fishing Loch Lubnaig in such
circumstances, and doleful indeed was old Davy,
our boatman, at our want of luck. About an hour
before we stopped, however, there was a break in
the clouds over Ben Ledi, and a broad strip of
light streaked across the loch. "Let's troll there,"
said Davy; and, sure enough, every time our
minnow went spinning across the bright part we
had a fish on the rod, until we caught nine in all.

＊   ＊   ＊

A friend and I were staying for a few days in
Lauder one April, our purpose being to fish the
Leader. The season was bitterly cold, and our
baskets were anything but prize ones. We had
not the consolation, meagre though it be, of
knowing that every fisher was alike unsuccessful,
for regularly each night there appeared at the

"Black Bull" a local "professional" who displayed nice baskets of from six to eight pounds of well-conditioned trout. How he got them was a mystery to us all, for the water was low and clear, and there was scarcely any sunshine to bring out the insect life of the streams. One morning, however, we got a glimpse of our friend's mode of procedure, which in some degree accounted for his baskets while the thermometer was at freezing-point. We were fishing the Leader about a mile above Lauder, when he passed us walking briskly, and now and then, for appearance sake, making a careless cast from the bank. All at once he laid down his rod and slipped quietly into the water: wading across to the other side, he stooped down, and with his arm bared he deliberately "guddled" a fine trout. This he repeated three times in the same stretch of water. The mystery of his baskets was cleared up now, entirely to our satisfaction, if not to his credit.

*   *

Two anglers whom we shall name respectively

A. and B. were fishing in a stream in Berwick-shire which was partly preserved. On coming to one of the preserved places they hesitated a while before they could make up their minds to turn back, but the gleam of rippling water and a plunge by a feeding trout was too much for them, and in a moment they had crossed the dividing fence. All went well for about half-an-hour, when round a bend of the river, a short distance in front of them, they saw a keeper coming. He evidently got his eye on them at the same moment, for he immediately quickened his pace.

What was to be done? "Let's pretend we are deaf and dumb," whispered A. No word further could be spoken; a nod of the head was all B. had time for ere the keeper accosted them.

"Did you not see the ticket down yonder?" the keeper enquired. A vacant stare, mutely inter-rogative, was all the answer he got from the culprits, who still kept casting away.

"I am saying, this water's preserved," shouted the keeper, in tones that might have been heard up at the "big" house.

Still there was no reply, but A. pointed sadly to his lips, signifying his sore affliction. A light seemed to dawn upon the keeper at this point. "Dummies baith, as I am a livin' man," he muttered.

Meanwhile B. had moved out into deep water, and was thus enabled to cast "far and fine" to the other side. He was so far successful that in a throw or two he raised a fine fish, but in the circumstances it was no wonder that he failed to hook it. He was not long in raising another, the keeper meanwhile fuming impotently on the bank, for both of the anglers, though "dumb" for the time being, were stalwart men, and force was out of the question. Fish number two, however, also escaped. This was too much for B.'s patience, who, forgetting his dumbness, and even becoming for the moment oblivious of the keeper's presence, exclaimed, "Confound it! missed him again!"—Tableau!

※   ※

One day, on Loch Leven, a friend caught three

trout at one cast. There were only three flies on his line, so that every one was successful. Strange to say, the fish caught complied with the three degrees of comparison, to this extent that they were respectively small, smaller, smallest, —for, unlike the average trout of this loch, the biggest one scarcely weighed half-a-pound. The boatman wisely managed to drop two of them back into the water as he took them off the hook.

※   ※   ※

It is not every one who can use a landing-net, though most people think they can. I remember one day, when the fish were scarce, that an officious friend made them scarcer by seizing the net from the boatman and making a plunge with it at the snout of the fish, thus severing my connection with a nice two-pound trout.

※   ※   ※

One day the late Mr John Mackenzie, of Manchester, who only fished for big trout—as we all do—was holding up a large trout which he had just netted in the Tweed below Walkerburn; but this act of triumph was his undoing, for the meshes of the net being worn, the trout fell through them into the water, breaking the line in his descent and making his escape.

＊

We are apt to take a pessimistic view of present-day fishing when we listen to the tales told of doughty deeds done by famous anglers on familiar streams in days that are not so very long gone by. Some of the following notes I heard from the lips of the late Adam Dryden; the others I have taken from his little book, 'Hints to Anglers'—a book long since out of print.

In April, 1858, on the Leader, Gala, and Tweed respectively, for 20 days' fishing, his take was 213 lbs., being an average of $10\frac{18}{40}$ lbs. each day. In May, 1858, on the Ettrick, Leader, Tweed, and Gala respectively, for 22 days' fishing, his take was 324 lbs., being an average of $14\frac{8}{11}$ lbs. each

day. In June, 1858, in nine days' fishing, as follows :—Seven days on the Gala, one day on the Leader, and—oilworks, please copy!—one day on the Almond, he had a total catch of 177 lbs., being an average of 19⅝ lbs. for each day.

The Gala takes are worthy of record, if only as a contrast to present - day baskets. They are as follows, the lure being May fly :—

June 1, Gala, above Stow,	...	...	10½ doz., 26 lbs.
„ 2, Gala, below Stow,	...	...	5 doz., 16 lbs.
„ 3, Gala, from Stow to Fountainhall,	12¼ doz., 36 lbs.
„ 5, Gala, same stretch as on the 3d,	9 doz., 24 lbs.
„ 6, Gala, below Bowland,	...	...	4½ doz., 11 lbs.
21, Gala (with worm),	...	7 doz., 20 lbs.

—making a nice average of 22⅛ lbs. for each day. As if this were not enough for our nerves, Dryden concludes—" The largest capture of trout, I believe, which I ever made was in the Leader in the spring of 1843, with fly. I did not note either the number or weight, but I filled three large baskets. They took the fly readily, even when the dressing was nearly all worn off it. In the Gala, in the month of June, I once killed 51 lbs. weight, a statement which I can prove by the testimony of credible witnesses."

After this, there is nothing for it but to lower the curtain, and sound "Lights out!"

*   *

When the sun shines, even the planets are unseen. So, 'mid the glory of classic scenes, the modest glens and their sparkling rivulets are overlooked and neglected.

> "The wind and the beam loved the rose,
>   But the rose loved one;
> For who recks the wind when it blows,
>   And loves not the sun?"

The unknown glens with their lonely cots have a history of their own, as interesting and absorbing as that of the glens whose fortune it has been to be discovered by the poets. Lovers of nature can easily recall spots they have come upon in their wanderings, as full of rare beauty as ever poet fancied; and yet, even the dwellers in the district were unaware of their existence. Sundhope is only typical of many of the lonely glens in the south of Scotland, and notably of those that intersect the valley of Yarrow.

SOLITUDE IN YARROW.

Lone vale of Sundhope, hid among the hills,
  A sense of peace steals o'er the wanderer's heart,
When, tired of city din and life's sad ills,
  He seeks thy bosom, ne'er again to part.

No storied fame entwines thy humble brow,
  No echo from the strifeful days of yore;
But only restfulness 'mid holm and howe,
  And heaven's own calm, through throbbing hearts to pour.

Without, may flame the world's dread passion-fires,
  And kingdoms rise and fall 'mid clamorous din;
But other thoughts thy silence vast inspires,
  Befitting immortality, and souls who heaven would win.

Embowered far up the glen a modest flower
  Once bloomed, untended and alone,
Nourished 'mid lonely scenes, a radiant dower
  Of innocence and beauty in her dark eyes shone.

But she is gone! and autumn winds sob low,
  The sunlight shines in joyous sheen no more;

And song-birds chant in measures sad and slow,
Attuned to hearts whose dream of life is o'er.

O solitude benign! a sense of bygone bliss
Thou brought'st, and, thrilling at thy touch, a chime
Comes wafted through the caves of memory, like kiss
Of first love, flushing all with ecstasy sublime!

AMONG THE SOURCES OF THE CLYDE

" There is grandeur in the birthplace of a mighty river,
Though round the fount be only wild heath-bells."

IX.

AMONG THE SOURCES OF THE CLYDE.

" Life hath its May, and is mirthful then ;
   The woods are vocal, and the flowers all odour.
   Its very blast hath mirth in't."

IT is now a long time since Mac., Wilson, and
the writer of this sketch spent a few days at
Leadhills, in south Lanarkshire. This village is
said to be the highest in the south of Scotland,
and is worthy of note for two or three other
things besides. For instance, it is remarkable
that within its precincts you never see, what is
so common elsewhere, the industrious fussy hen,
nor are your morning dreams disturbed by the
clarion notes of some too wakeful chanticleer.
The crushed quartz from the mines is used for
garden - paths and flower - borders, and looks very

nice; but, being much impregnated with lead, this same quartz is death to the foraging poultry.

The folk of the village are a very intelligent set of people, and having had a capital library presented to them long before such institutions were as common or as popular as they are now, they have always taken pride in keeping it in a high state of efficiency. It was in this village that Allan Ramsay was born, and where he spent the first fifteen years of his life. As he sings of himself—

> " Of Crawfurd-muir, born in Leadhills,
> Where mineral springs Glengoner fills ;
> Which joins sweet flowing Clyde."

We had duly seen the lions of Leadhills—had been down a mine, and along a " level," and had secured as many geological " specimens " as the railway company were likely to let go free as passengers' luggage. We had also been as far as Wanlockhead to see the Duke's Mines, and had seen part of the process by which silver is extracted from lead, the other part being a secret. Naturally,

after this effort to improve our minds, being yet in
our teens, we began to sigh for "green fields and
pastures new."

There were two fishing - rods amongst us, and
we tried our skill in the Elvan and Glengonar
waters, which both flow near Leadhills; but the
trout had decidedly the best of the sport. In
the circumstances it was quite soothing · to be
told that it was not altogether our want of skill
that kept our basket so painfully clean, but that
the presence in the streams of the water pumped
out of the mines had a good deal to do with our
non-success. Essence of lead was not more nourish-
ing to trout than it was to poultry.

"Let's cross the Lowthers to the Clyde," said
Wilson, who was of an adventurous nature, and
who, since then, has had plenty of scope for its
exercise among the backwoods of America. This
proposal being hailed with acclamation, as anything
that is novel ever is by the young, we duly prepared
for a long walk and a big day's fishing among the
Lowther streams that flow to the Clyde.

The next morning, after having been duly warned

to avoid the disused pit-mouths on our way, we
started about 7 o'clock to cross the moor and climb
the slope of the hill that leads to the famous Enterkin Pass. We had no map, and were in the happy
condition of not knowing where we were going,
and in the mood of caring even less. Had we not
a whole day before us, and a good Scotch tongue
in our head? And then, what a zest is given
to an outing by the anticipation of the unexpected!
This is not a Hibernicism, but a subtle charm in
healthy life.

The name " Lowther Hills," though frequently
applied to the entire mountainous district stretch-
ing between the counties of Ayr, Lanark, Dumfries,
and Peebles, more correctly belongs to that range
running north-east from Leadhills, and south-west
from the same point towards the sources of the
Powtrail.

These hills are impressive features in the landscape, and are by no means to be despised, even
by admirers of the lofty Bens farther north. The
"Green Lowther" actually attains a height of
2400 feet, while, taken all over, the other summits

reach an altitude of over 2000 feet. In crossing
these hills to the Clyde, we had no need to diverge
so far from the direct route as to be carried down
Enterkin Pass into Dumfriesshire. But youthful
walking tours are like school-boy short cuts home;
the sauntering detour is the best of it.

The remarkable gorge of Enterkin is seldom
visited except by shepherds, or by passing anglers;
and yet, there are few glens in the south of Scotland more worthy of contemplation. This arises
not merely because it possesses natural features
of grandeur, fitted to inspire the mind with senti-
ments of awe and admiration, but also because
there are historical associations hovering over the
glen, such as no patriot should willingly let die.
Our footpath was a mere sheep-walk, high up on
the slope of the precipitous hill, which descended
to the bed of the brawling burn below. Up where
we were, there was mist; but as we wended our
way towards the Covenanters' Spring, we left the
mist behind us, and far in front we could see the
sun shining brightly in Nithsdale.

Resting at the spring—as in duty we were bound

to do—and looking back towards the summit of the pass, it was easy to picture how a conventicle might be held here, even though the pursuing dragoons looked helplessly on from their vantage-ground above.   Indeed, tradition narrates that an incident thus imagined actually happened.   Having continued our descent until we had traversed two-thirds of the pass, we crossed the burn and pre-pared to climb the "stey goyle," a very steep but less lofty part of the range.   Tradition has been at work here also, and tells that Captain Grier rode, or rather slid, down the hillside on horseback, when pursuing some of the hill folks in the killing times, and that the marks of the horse's hoofs are still to be seen.   Not being called upon to ex-press an opinion as to the probability of this story, we dispersed to search for the cave where so many of the men of Sanquhar found a hiding-place in troublous times, 'particulars of which events one may find fully recorded in Simpson's interesting volume, 'Gleanings among the Mountains.'

Not knowing, however, which was the cave in question, we next turned our attention to a thorough exploration of the rocky burn of Enterkin. How strangely diverse are the ways of men in viewing a stream! One sees before him running water— a necessity of life — somewhat cold maybe, occasionally refreshing, and in all circumstances strictly complying with the law of gravity. But it has no story to tell him. Another sees, not water, but an inhabited world, with caverns wherein genii dwell, and yellow sands whereon the water-sprites hold their moonlight revels. To him the mossy bank becomes an elfland hunting-ground; and the plashing of the tiny waterfall sounds to his ear as *carillons* of joy bells celebrating the festivities of countless naiads. I cannot deny myself the privilege of quoting a very interesting stanza bearing upon such reflections, which heads chapter xii. of ' The Monastery.'

> " There's something in that ancient superstition
> Which, erring as it is, our fancy loves.
> The spring that, with its thousand crystal bubbles,
> Bursts from the bosom of some desert rock
> In secret solitude, may well be deem'd
> The haunt of something purer, more refined,
> And mightier than ourselves."

We had a pretty stiff climb before we reached the top of the hill, and our unanimous verdict was that it fully merited the name of "stey." The provoking element lay in the fact that though we had come so far, the source of the Clyde was as great a mystery as ever. Wilson, who was our guide, held on farther west, which, as we afterwards found, only led us away from our destination. But the day was bright, and our hearts were light; so it was, on! and tally ho! once more.

We must have gone through the pass of Dalveen, and had not known it; for by-and-by we came to a quaint old church and a quiet churchyard—no less a place than Durisdeer. There is quite a Yarrow flavour about this name, which signifies "the door of the forest," but, as every reader knows, the history as well as the romance of this district is second to none in Scotland. How impressive is an auld kirkyard—one of the kind that has no wall round it, but where the grass just merges in the heather! There is such an old-time lonesomeness about the place that you are

fain to hold your breath and tread softly. The
very grass grows pensively; and the few gowans
and blue-bells, and, it may be, a cowslip or two,
that have sprung up within the shelter of the
tombstones, seem to be mutely appealing to you
to remove them to the other side of the brae,
where the sun shines longer, and where the young
lambs frisk and play. These reflections are inten-
sified when you remember that sleeping here in
the shadow of the hills are men who had convic-
tions strong enough to be suffered for—men who
sought the shelter of the moss-hags on the moors,
or in the wildest recesses of yon glen, that their
homes and kindred might be scathless because of
their absence.

From the time we had left Leadhills until the
hour of noon, we had not met a single person
from whom we could glean any information as to
our road. But while exploring the kirkyard we
were hailed by an old man, evidently the beadle,
who, in answer to our enquiries, told us that we
were "a' wrang thegither." We should have
turned south-east instead of south-west when we

emerged from the Enterkin if we ever wished to see the Clyde! This afforded us a good joke at Wilson's expense; but without further delay we retraced our steps along what I afterwards learned was a famous Roman road. An old writer says that "this road went up Nithsdale on the east side of the Nith, passing by the village of Thorn-hill, and crossing Carron water a little above its influx into the Nith. From this passage the road continued its course in a northerly direction past a Roman fort in a remarkable pass above the kirk of Durisdeer; from this place it pushed through the hill by the defile called the wall-path, and went down the east side of Powtrail water to its confluence with the Dair."

We had a good bit of moor to cross before we saw, coming down a valley on our right, a some-what sluggish stream of considerable volume. This proved to be the "Powtrail," one of the chief feeders of the Clyde. Rising in the southern Lowthers, this stream is seven miles long, and besides, it receives several nice tributaries in its course. We saw then, what I have often seen since, that it is a stream teeming with trout and grayling. Many a pleasant day have I had in its quiet valley, and I can fancy few places better suited for an angler's holiday.

Although this stream has been greatly fished since the time I speak of, there seems to be as many trout as ever. The last time I tried my skill in it was about two years ago, early in September. I had left Edinburgh in the morning by the 6.50 train for Elvanfoot, but owing to some delay at Carstairs it was 9.40 before we arrived there. After an hour's walk I reached the place on the Powtrail where I thought it best to make my first·cast. This was at a point a few yards below where the Peden Burn joins the main stream. The flies I selected were, "teal and black," "woodcock," and a grouse hackle, all of a small size, the water being low and clear. Not ·long after beginning I had the luck to land a fine yellow trout of 1 lb. 2 oz., which feat had·a wonderful effect on my hopes, as well as upon things in .general. These expectations were not disappointed by the sport that followed, so that,

I

shortly after three o'clock, when I began to think
of my long walk back to catch the five o'clock
train — I having fished up stream — the basket
weighed fully 7 lbs., which I considered not bad
sport in low water for five hours' work.

I had just come to the determination to make
for the railway station, when a fisher joined me
from up stream, and of course we had a chat.
It was then I learned that he had gone over the
same part of the river that I had been fishing
early in the morning, and had been up the water
fully five miles. He somewhat patronisingly said
that for "shop flees" my take was not bad; but
when he showed me his own basket I easily saw
how my 7 lbs. appeared to him of so little
account. His creel was full to the lid, there being
no less than 25 lbs. of trout and grayling packed
tightly within. Of course he had been at it by
daylight, but it was not his early start that had
filled the creel, but rather his lures, which were
just natural flies caught at the river side.

But to return to my first experience here. No
time was lost by Wilson and myself in getting

our rods in order and making a start. But—of
course "but"—the sun was bright, and the water
was low, and the banks were high, and we did
not wade; and so no fisher need be told that our
baskets were light. It was here that Mac. came
into evidence in quite an original character.
Thus, while we were doing our little best at one
part he would go on in front, as he said, "to
look for a better place." Whenever he saw a
shoal of fish he would stand on the edge of the
bank waving his arms and gesticulating wildly for
us to come on, for, as he shouted, "here they
are!" The result of this frantic conduct was
simply to drive every fish within fifty yards of him
out of sight and past all chance of being taken.

Being thus compelled to skip long stretches of
water, we soon passed the large farm called the
Nunnery, and arrived at the point where the
Powtrail joins the Daur. This meeting of the
waters is usually spoken of as a union, but it
is a union by absorption; for the Daur from its
source to this point has had a run of fourteen
miles, and is now an imposing river, quite able to

swallow the Powtrail and never say a word about it. Indeed, this is the real Clyde, although the little burn of that name does not enter the river until you are within a mile of Elvanfoot. The Daur, or, as I would call it, the Upper Clyde, rises in Queensberry Hill, in Dumfriesshire, and in its course receives six or seven burns of considerable size. The name Clyde signifies " wan water." What a contrast—the Clyde at Nunnery and the Clyde at Broomielaw! It is well, for rivers and people alike, that they do not know what is awaiting them.

There are few streams in the south-west of Scotland that have as many fish in them as the Clyde. For, besides trout, it is the home of the grayling. True, there are no salmon, but then there are no parr; and to a humble trout-fisher that is an important element in our choice of a stream. Unless in times of flood, when, as the local people say, "Clyde is oot," the takes of trout are not very large, though occasionally big baskets of grayling are got with minnow. Two things seem to me to account for this. First, because the banks are so high that it is almost impossible to cast without being seen, unless you are wading; second, because there are so many fishers on the water all the year round that the fish have become extremely shy. The Clyde is much in need of a close time. I remember speaking with a local fisher while waiting for a train, and he told me that he had got "a grand basket o' trout last New Year's Day!" Of course it is ostensibly to fish for grayling that men go out to the river in mid-winter, but, unfortunately, they take anything else they can get.

It was with none of these thoughts in our minds that my friends and I followed the stream down the pastoral valley of the Upper Clyde. Undoubtedly it is a charming place, and were it not so far from Glasgow and Edinburgh, would have many a citizen in need of rest resorting thither for a day amongst its silvery streams. Before we realised it, the sun had set behind the Lowthers, and dusk was upon us. How to get home was the question, but it was easier asked than answered. Mac.'s quick eye caught sight of some one going along a road that lay on our left, so we all crossed the moor to meet him. It was a considerable relief to learn from our friend, who was evidently a shepherd on an adjoining farm, that we were only two miles from Elvanfoot. Thanking our informant, we bundled up our rods and stepped briskly out for home. Leadhills lies five miles west of Elvanfoot, and so our return journey was up the valley of the Elvan. But ere we saw the lights of the village, ten o'clock had come and gone, and we knew that our several friends there would be in no ordinary state of anxiety regarding our fate. They keep very early hours in Leadhills; perhaps that will account for the fact that I saw on a stone in their kirkyard that one of the inhabitants was 137 years old when he died.

When at last we entered the village, great was our surprise to find little groups of men standing here and there on the road. Still greater was our surprise when we learned that some of the men had ropes, and that they were just about to start over the moor in search of us wanderers!

THE ANGLER'S HOPE.

What recks it, though they tell us times have changed,
  That streams are waning, and sport's record light,
That in days bygone giants of the angle ranged
  By loch and stream, all conquering, with Trojan might?

What though their sport ne'er failed from morn till night;
  Their streams ran ever full, their skies gleamed ever blue;
While breezes from the mountains played but soft and light,
  And clouds had never shadows, and hearts beat ever true.

Does Tweed not flow as silvery to the northern sea
  As in the days when troopers marshall'd on her shore?
Does Clyde not wander 'mong her hills as free
  As when brave Wallace wight the sword for freedom bore?

Do lovers meet no more by Ettrick's leafy shaws,
  And Gala no more run 'neath hill-pent Fountainhall?
Has time reversed great Nature's heaven-given laws,
  And desolation grim sit brooding over all?

Have birks by lonely burnsides stunted grown,
  And heather on the hills a' wede away?
Has Yarrow lost her charm, and are for ever flown
  The larks that high at heaven's gate hailed opening day?

'Tis but a fancy! change lurks in the doubter's breast!
  Impassively the hills behold our evanescent dreams;
Their fronts point heavenward, where the pilgrims rest
  Who loved their fellowship and besung their streams.

Our land was made for heroes! doubting men
  Can never roam her hills or sing her world-wide fame;
The breezes from the Highland loch and Lowland glen
  Shall ever stir the angler's heart to patriotic flame.

MEGGAT AND HER TRIBUTARIES

" My teachers are the hills; no truth that feigns
A subtle wisdom drawn from weary brains
                    With laboured care,
But nature's teaching, that from daisied sod
To lark - sung heights can find the love of God
                    Plain written everywhere."
                    —*J. B.'s ' Retreat in Yarrow.'*

X.

MEGGAT AND HER TRIBUTARIES.

HAVING lived for several summers on the banks of the Meggat, I have naturally a warm side to it. This is not to be wondered at, for it is a charming stream, considered either historically or from a picturesque point of view. It is seven miles long, and flows through a lonely valley, almost destitute of trees. It has all the aspects peculiar to Yarrow, and has had hard lines in having been overlooked and neglected so long by the poets.

As a fishing stream it ranks high; for not only is it well stocked with trout, native to itself, but it has, in addition, frequent migrants from the loch who add the charm of unexpectedness to your capture when you get à big fellow. Many sea-trout

and bull-trout ascend the waters in late autumn;
and such of them as escape the leister make for
the sea in early spring, and you not infrequently
come upon an occasional one as it is resting in
Yarrow on its way down. There are some remarkably deep pools in Meggat, in which big
trout from the loch take up their quarters.
These rovers have all a history, and are noted
for their rapid growth. Thus, the first time you
are told about them they may be said to weigh
two pounds; but, ere a few days pass, you are
confidently assured that he is " four pounds at
least."

The Meggat has some peculiarities of its own
in times of flood, especially in its lower waters.
For instance, owing to the presence of large
quantities of peat in solution, you can seldom get
a trout to rise to a fly until two days after the
spate. Then is the time for fishing its upper
reaches and tributaries.

The Meggat aptly prefigures life, if looked at
in three stages. The upper waters may be taken
to represent youth—

" Whyles ow'r a linn the burnie plays,
    As through the glen it wimpl't;
    Whyles round a rocky scaur it strays,
    Whyles in a wiel it dimpl't."

The mid-stream flows steadily and purpose-like,
as manhood faces duties and difficulties; and the
lower water, after emerging from the rocky barriers
below the island, flows with increasing velocity to
the lake; as old age longs for, and would hasten
unto, the rest of eternity. Perhaps the best impression of this district will be got if the reader
accompanies me up one side of the valley and down
the other, and so take all the tributaries in the
order we approach them. Proceeding then from
the mouth of the Meggat to its source, the first
stream we come to on our right is Henderland
Burn. This stream, though it has several romantic
falls, bulks larger in history than it does in nature.
The last time we saw the glen we found the knoll
where the castle once stood occupied by the tents
of the Teviotdale Camping Club. They are a
jovial set of fellows, and wake the valley at night-
fall with the strains of " Teribus."

Dow Linn is a beautiful spot which has been often celebrated in song, because of its tragic connection with the death of Peris Cockburn, the outlaw, and that of his wife Marjorie. There being no trout above the falls, the present writer has frequently carried them up to the higher pools from the pools below the falls, and it gave much pleasure to find that they were taking kindly to their new quarters. Judge of our chagrin on hearing that this summer an angler from Innerleithen, with that thoughtlessness that has so often brought about restriction where none previously existed, had come down the stream from the top and cleaned out every pool!

The nature of this stream in its upper reaches is sluggish and turbid, oozing out of crumbling peaty soil. Sheep are often smothered here in winter, a very fatal part being the pools of the east fork near the source. Returning to the Meggat valley, and still ascending, we next come to Glengaber Burn. This stream rises about four miles from this point, at the Bitch Craig, near the source of the Manor. Like all the tributaries of the Meggat, the Glengaber varies greatly in its volume—the water, unless when there is a flood, being locked up in dark, deep pools. Gold is found at certain parts of the stream, and we have seen both finger- and ear-rings which had been made from the unalloyed metal as it had been picked out of the fissures in the rocks.

Wending our way for a mile farther upwards, we come to Craigierig Burn, a stream much the same in every respect as the Glengaber, excepting that there is no gold. Half-a-mile farther west we come to Cramilt Burn, where it flows past the ruins of the old hunting - lodge of the Scottish Court. We are tempted to speak of the old times, when gay cavalcades rode from the courtyard of the castle to chase the deer which roamed in such numbers in the adjoining forest of Rodono. Specially do we think of that last occasion when Mary and Darnley followed the famous stag which rose at Syart ("*See the Hart!*"), and which, after being chased for miles, escaped by taking the famous "hart's leap" near Ettrick. If you doubt the legend, are not the stones put up to mark the spot standing till this day?' More-over, are we not told further by the historian that the royal pair were disappointed that the spoils of this visit did not amount to more than "auchteen score o' deer." But it is the physical features of the district that we are treating of at present, and not its historical.

Proceeding onwards, we next come to Ling-hope Burn, which has several deep pools and one very high fall. The last tributary of the Meggat, which flows in from the hills on the north-west side of the valley, is the Wylie Burn. Although dark pools are plentiful enough in the lower waters, yet the middle section is distinguished by a remarkable series of cascades which slide to a level lower than the upper section by at least eighty or a hundred feet. The gorge through which the water falls is pretty wide, and the hills on either side have their slopes clad at autumn time in the loveliest heather. In every crevice of the cliffs the blue-bell, the ivy, and innumerable flowering-plants are rooted; while the dwarf rowan tree, the foxglove, and the bracken grow profusely wherever they can find a foothold. To come upon such a charming scene unexpectedly is intensely enjoyable, and you marvel that such a picturesque spot should have been left for you to discover.

Above the Wylie, as far as to the ridge at Meggatstone, there are no other tributaries except-ing some small "sykes" which flow through the moors. We cross the river, therefore, and retrace our steps downwards towards the loch, coming soon thereafter to Winterhope Burn. This is the largest tributary of the Meggat, and is the chief agent in giving character and colour to the waters of the river. Excepting in its middle course, where it flows over granite rocks for nearly a mile, the "Wintrup" winds through flat, mossy moors. Rising about five miles from its junction with the Meggat, and about a quarter of a mile east from Loch Skene, it would be difficult to imagine a drearier scene than its upper waters present to the eye. Great fields of peat, inter-sected by ridges of heath, and hemmed in by high bent-clad hills, form the gathering-ground of

K

this stream, while at its source there is a chain
of black, slimy pools. Trout do not seem to like
such water, and it is not until you descend the
valley for nearly two miles that they are met
with.   The vale is well named Winterhope, and
dreary indeed must be the dark months of the
year to the shepherd, his wife, and son, who are
the only inhabitants of the glen.   The trout in
Winterhope are much larger than the average
size of those in any other tributary of the Meggat.
If the burn is caught just on the rise, the angler
will be astonished at the size as well as the
number of the trout that find their way to his
creel.   I remember one morning setting out for
Loch Skene, *via* Winterhope.   As I came in sight
of the latter, just after rounding the hill from
Shielhope, the water was of a blackish colour and
gurgling in an unusual manner.   It was on the
rise.   The rain and wind had hitherto been in
my face; but now, owing to the great bays in
the surrounding hills, it went round so that it
blew up stream.   Not having got Winterhope in
this condition before, I could not resist trying

my luck, even though Loch Skene had to wait. Selecting a "blackcock hackle with a red body," and a "pheasant wing with orange body," I cast over a nice frothy pool. In a moment I had two good trout on, which were both landed after some difficulty. The next cast was equally successful, though only one trout was encreeled this time. ·But not to speak too minutely of the sport, I may say that before I reached the shepherd's house I had thirteen pounds of fine trout. As my old friend said when he saw them—"The best basket since the days Wullie Richardson used to fish Wint'rup."

Emerging from Winterhope at Meggatknowes, and once more proceeding down the valley, ere long Shielhope Burn is reached. The chief features of this stream are narrow pools, of considerable depth, and a spouting cascade, with a fall of about twenty-five feet. The trout of the Meggat never got up the stream beyond this fall until the late Earl of Wemyss told his gamekeeper to carry some above the obstruction. How this was eventually done is an interesting fact in natural history. At first the trout placed above the fall were naturally taken from the Meggat, but, much to the keeper's chagrin and annoyance, they invariably made for their native stream again, refusing to make a new home in Shielhope Burn. In his dilemma the keeper applied to the Earl for advice, and was surprised to be told that he had been acting quite contrary to the nature and habits of the fish he thought he knew so well, for they will never stay in a stream whose source is higher than their own. It was an easy matter after learning this to take them from the Linghope Burn, whose waters come from higher springs, and since then trout have remained and increased in Shielhope. It should be mentioned that, like all the streams that flow into the Meggat from the south-west, this water is very brown in colour, and the trout have a dark bronze-like hue.

The last tributary of any note on this side is the Syart Burn, and a little one very near it rejoicing in the suggestive name of the Dirthope. These streams have all the characteristics of those already mentioned, excepting that though

they are smaller they have some large trout in
their pools. They are seldom visited save by
the shepherd of the adjoining hirsel, Mr P. Wood
(who knows Meggat better than most visitors), and
the present writer.

We cannot conclude our sketch of Meggat without speaking of the worth of the dwellers in the
valley. Perhaps some idea of what I mean may
be gathered from a characteristic remark made by
a highly respected shepherd, well known to visitors
and residents alike. "James," said a farmer to
him, "I see Mr A—— over at Peebles is wanting
a shepherd, but," he continued, "the applicant
must produce characters from his last three
masters." "Aweel," said James, "that wadna
dae for me, for I hae only been wi' ae maister a'
my days!"

IN MEGGAT.

We sing the charms of Meggat vale,
  Enshrined in song and story olden ;
A mellow light glints on the stream,
  The hills repose in sunlight golden.

The pensive autumn brings to mind
  The days of Scotland's ancient glory,
When Cramalt's halls rang with the shout
  Of huntsmen, stirr'd by minstrel's story.

Far in Rodono forest dark,
  The echoing bugle-note rose high,
And Wint'rup, drear, to Linghope linns,
  Repeated oft the wolf's dread cry.

The boar cleuch in Glengaber glen
  Recalls the days of Royal sport,
When balefires gleamed and banners waved
  On outlaw's tower and vassal's court.

Gone tower and stag, gone wild boar grim,
  Gone trooper's shout, and reiver's tread ;
All gone ! save stream, and burn, and linn,
  And mountains bold, and cliffs of dread.

Yet soughs of eld will o'er us steal,
  As by the Meggat's banks we wander,
And sound with thought harmonious blend,
  Life's lights and shadows as we ponder.

An old-time glamour haunts the spot,
  Though gone be all the pomp and glare;
For farm, and lodge, and shepherd's cot
  Shield hearts too true for envy's snare.

And children's voices blythe ring out
  By glen, and burn, and peaceful braes;
While fisher's rod, and shepherd's crook
  Supplant the arms of bygone days.

Then sing we Meggat's vale and stream,
  With Syart lone, and Cramalt grand;
When life grows drear, still would we dream
  Of golden days in Henderland!

ON THE ETTRICK

" Ettricke Foreste is a feir foreste,
In it grows manie a semelie tree;
There's hart and hynd, and dae and rae,
And of a' wild bestis grete plentie."
                                    —*Old Ballad.*

ON THE ETTRICK.

Who has not heard of Ettrick Shaws, or of the Ettrick Shepherd? Yet of all who have heard of either, it is remarkable how few ever dream of penetrating into the lovely valley, so fascinating in song and story.

The stately Ettrick Pen sits undisturbed in solitary glory at the farthest limits of the glen; and the brownies of Bodesbeck Law may carry on their pranks for good or evil, safe alike from the scream of the railway whistle or the bugle of the stage-coach.

The river Ettrick is about thirty miles long, and presents many features of interest, both of a historic and of an artistic nature; but as it is its features as a trouting stream that we have to

do with at present, we defer the consideration of
the other points till a future time. As an angling
stream it used to have a deservedly high character,
but its stock of trout has been much reduced of
late years by unfair fishers, who do their work
with nets in the summer nights. These plunderers,
it is right to say, are not residents, but are visitors
from distant towns. In the winter season there
are usually many salmon and sea trout in the
Ettrick, but even these are scarcer than in former
times, in consequence of the greater difficulty the
fish have in getting over the caulds at Selkirk and
Philiphaugh. In the upper parts, which are too
remote for being strictly watched, "burning the
water" is indulged in with impunity, and that
serves to thin the "redds" to some extent. The
natives of Ettrick are adroit with the leister, and,
unfortunately, they don't distinguish between trout
and "fish" when using it. Hence the trout fishing has fallen off when compared with the baskets
of forty years ago. I remember one of the resident
fishers bewailing this fact to me; but he also in
a manner put his finger on the cause, for he re-

marked slyly, " I daursay I have mysel' to blame, for when I cam' here forty years sin', I was gey keen on the fishin'; so, when I gaed oot i' the mornin' for a walk doun by Thirlstane, I wad tak' a bit cleek in my pooch, juist to tie on to my stick, div 'e sey? An' when I saw a biggish troot lyin' near the bank, of coorse I juist raxed ow'r and cleekit him oot!"

The Ettrick differs in some notable points from most of the rivers in the south of Scotland. Thus, granite and whinstone abounding throughout the district, we find here and there in the course of the stream that some very striking effects are produced by the water rushing through rocky gorges, across which it would be easy for you to leap. Then, at Cossarshill and Ettrickbridge End, the water flows over broad ledges of whinstone, forming deep pools of olive hue, in which it is said some salmon lie all the year round. The rocky and pebbly nature of the river frequently upsets the calculations of the most experienced anglers; for it is not uncommon to find that, in a few hours after a flood—just when other streams are coming into ply—the water has pretty nearly run off, and the Ettrick has fallen to nearly its normal level. On the other hand, if there has been rain up among the hills, it generally rises quicker than its neighbouring streams, so that in going out after a few showers, in the hope of finding the stream in good trim, and the trout in a taking mood, you are surprised to find the river in flood, owing to the rapid discharge of the surface water from the burns.

The trout of the Ettrick are somewhat dark in colour, and, from having to fight against strong currents, they are lively fish—a six ounce fellow will give more play than one twice his weight in a slow-running stream. Anglers on rivers usually rail against an east wind; but I always found that an east wind was the best for fishing Ettrick— I fancy not only because by it you could fish entirely up stream, but also, because by it the surface of the deep gorge-like pools was nicely rippled.

The most successful fisher of these deep pools that I met with was one of the residents who

fished them with minnow, and always in the
evening, preferring before all other conditions a low
water. There is one very remarkable feature common to all the streams flowing into Ettrick above
Tushielaw, and that is the prevalence of falls or
linns throughout their course, but especially near
their source. Some of these linns are very striking
features in an otherwise moorland scene; but
they are not so interesting to anglers, for reasons
to be afterwards mentioned.

I once spent a long fishing holiday in Ettrick.
It was the year of "the caterpillar plague," and
famous for its drought. As I drove from Selkirk,
my first impressions of the tributaries of the
Ettrick were that they were as apocryphal as
the snakes of Iceland! Streams that bulk pretty
largely on the map seemed nothing but ancient
watercourses, with only stones and boulders left
to show where water once had been. In these
circumstances we did little fishing for a week or
two, but we had some charming walking tours
instead, and got to know the hospitable dwellers
in the several farm-houses above the Tima very

well indeed. There are some glorious views to be had from the hills on either side of the valley, while from the "Pen" the panorama that lies around is unsurpassed in the south of Scotland.

The primitive ways of the people and of the district remind you of some of Boston's remarks in his 'Autobiography,' so little have manners and customs seemed to change since his time. The postman goes no farther than Ramsaycleuch, which is eighteen miles from Selkirk, but the glen is nearly ten miles longer than that, so if you are not at the post office to get your letters, some one may kindly take them on as far as his house, where they lie until a passer-by offers to carry them a mile or two farther on still, until by-and-by you hear there is something waiting for you "doun the waeter." So, after all, there is something to be said for modern progress.

No sweeter nook could well be fancied than Ettrick Kirk and its kirkyard; and by Scotsmen the last resting-place of Boston, Hogg, and Tibbie Shiel can never be passed unvisited. Worthy James Hogg! We often think that Lockhart did

him but scant justice; perhaps because he did not understand him; but we never can pass the spot, a few yards down the road east from the church, where the cottage in which he was born once stood, without pausing to sing a tributary verse from one of his beautiful lyrics. To many visitors the manse has long been synonymous with Scottish hospitality.

Having fished every tributary of Ettrick from Tushielaw to its source, I am tempted to dwell upon their merits; but as many guide-books now exist for that alone, I shall only speak of one or two streams that illustrate the features peculiar to the rest. After passing Tushielaw, as you ascend the valley you will come to a stream called Hope-house Burn, which joins the Ettrick from your right. The only time I fished it was once after I had tried my fortune up Kirkhouse Burn, behind the manse. I crossed the hill in a north-easterly direction, and came down upon the Hope at its source. On seeing it I felt sure that I was in luck that day, for no streamlet ever had more coy wavelets disappearing under deep overhanging

L

banks, or more musical, fascinating falls and shady pools. These I fished carefully for nearly a mile, but not a trout was to be seen. This was incomprehensible, and upset all my previous experience; but I was not left long in wonder, for soon the sound of falling water was heard, and presently, as I rounded a projecting knoll, I came upon a deep ravine into which the water fell. It was one of these linns to which reference has already been made, and so the mystery of my non-success was solved — for no fish that ever swam could mount a fall thirty feet high. Thus I had been fishing for more than an hour in beautiful water, possessing every grace fitted to catch a fisher's fancy—except the fish. In the pool below this fall I caught, at my first cast, a fine trout of nearly a pound weight; and on the next half mile of water I got some remarkably large fish, considering the size of the stream. Indeed, I was much struck with the fact that on all the tributaries of the Ettrick the fish were much heavier than those usually got in similar burns elsewhere. But a further point which I scored from my experience on this stream was, "never try to steal a march upon the Ettrick burns from the rear;" and it was well that I laid this lesson to heart, for, without exception, all the burns in the upper part of the valley were marked by the outstanding features of high cliffs and landslips in their higher reaches.

The Tima is the only other tributary that I would notice here, because, excepting the Yarrow, it is the largest stream that the Ettrick receives. Rising in the south at the watershed in Eskdalemuir, it has a course of six miles, and receives on its way four fairly large feeders. Many people consider the sport to be got in this stream superior to that of the Ettrick, and certainly, from my experience of it, I should say that the fish are larger in the average. The banks of the stream are quite free from trees or bushes, and I know of few places where you can get such an uninterrupted cast as on the Tima. There was one natural feature about half-way up the valley that took my fancy greatly. It was a broad strath of granite rock which had been laid bare by centuries of floods; and, standing in one of the hollows among the rocks, it was easy for you to think you stood amid the ruins of an engulfed city, all traces of whose inhabitants had been lost. The river runs to the left of these rocks in a narrow channel, and at one place there is a short fall which causes an eddy at the neck of a deep pool. On one side of this pool there is a thick wall of granite, and during the ages that the eddy has surged here it has managed to scoop out of the solid rock a beautifully finished alcove of considerable size and perfect form.

The liberty granted by Lord Napier and other proprietors in the district deserves to be put on record. This, with the courtesy and kindness of the people, makes the memory of a holiday in Ettrick a joy for ever.

ADIEU!

The stream gives forth a sadder song
  Than what it sang a month ago;
The hills are flecked with russet brown,
  Instead of summer's after-glow.

The swallows from the eaves have flown,
  The lapwing from the moor;
The wild swan southward wings the loch;
  The robin seeks the door.

High on the hills the sad ewes bleat;
  The wild goats haunt the vale;
The lowing of the kine at eve
  Sounds sadly on the gale.

All speak of change and pensiveness,
  Which finds its reflex in our heart,
For ere another day has fled,
  We from this loved vale must depart.

AU REVOIR!

But fancy brighter thoughts can borrow
  From every echo up the glen;
And sad hearts bear the present sorrow,
  In faith that "summer comes again!"

PRINTED BY

GEORGE LEWIS AND SON, SELKIRK.

GEORGE LEWIS & SON'S PUBLICATIONS.

REMINISCENCES OF YARROW.

By the Late JAMES RUSSELL, D.D., Minister of Yarrow. With Preface by Professor CAMPBELL FRASER. Twenty Illustrations by TOM SCOTT, A.R.S.A., and Portrait of the Author. Price, 5/- nett. Edition-de-luxe (limited), 12/6 nett. Copies may still be had.

THE COUNTRY AND CHURCH OF THE CHEERYBLE

BROTHERS. By the Rev. W. HUME ELLIOT, Ramsbottom. Fifty Fine Process Engravings, including Full-page Portraits of the Cheeryble Brothers. Price, 7/6 nett.

AUNT JANET'S LEGACY TO HER NIECES.

By Mrs JANET BATHGATE. With Full-page Illustrations, including Portrait of the Author. Price, 2/6 nett.

RIVERSIDE RAMBLES OF AN EDINBURGH

ANGLER. By DUNCAN FRASER, First President of the Edinburgh Saturday Angling Club. Six Full-page Engravings from Special Sketches by TOM SCOTT, A.R.S.A. Price, 3/6.

CRAIGMILLAR AND ITS ENVIRONS.

With Notices of the Topography, Natural History, and Antiquities of the District. By TOM SPEEDY. With numerous Illustrations. Price, 6/6.

WALTER WATHERSHANKS' ADVENTURES AT

LAMMAS FAIR. With Twelve Clever Illustrations from Original Sketches, and Pictorial Cover. Price, 6d.

TO BE HAD OF ALL BOOKSELLERS.

www.ingramcontent.com/pod-product-compliance
Lightning Source LLC
Chambersburg PA
CBHW030606040726
47497CB00008B/2876